COMMUNITY
LAND TRUST
APPLICATIONS
IN URBAN
NEIGHBORHOODS

A Common Ground Monograph

COMMUNITY LAND TRUST APPLICATIONS IN URBAN NEIGHBORHOODS

John Emmeus Davis
Line Algoed
María E. Hernández-Torrales

EDITORS

TERRA NOSTRA PRESS
Madison, Wisconsin, USA

TERRA NOSTRA PRESS

Center for Community Land Trust Innovation
3146 Buena Vista Street
Madison, Wisconsin, USA 53704

Publisher's Cataloging-in-Publication Data

Names: Davis, John Emmeus, editor. | Algoed, Line, editor. | Hernández-Torrales, María E., editor.
Title: Community land trust applications in urban neighborhoods. /
John Emmeus Davis ; Line Algoed ; María E. Hernández-Torrales, editors.
Series: Common Ground Monographs
Description: Includes bibliographical references. | Madison, WI: Terra Nostra Press, 2020.
Identifiers: Library of Congress Control Number: 2020920161 |
ISBN: 978-1-7344030-7-7 (paperback) | ISBN: 978-1-7344030-8-4 (ebook)
Subjects: LCSH Land trusts. | Land tenure. | Land use. | Land use, Urban. | Nature conservation. |
Landscape protection. | Sustainable development. | Economic development—Environmental aspects. |
City planning—Environmental aspects. | Community development. | Urban ecology (Sociology) |
BISAC POLITICAL SCIENCE / Public Policy / City Planning & Urban Development | LAW / Housing
& Urban Development | BUSINESS & ECONOMICS / Development / Sustainable Development |
SOCIAL SCIENCE / Sociology / Urban
Classification: LCC KF736.L3 W49 2020 | DDC 333.2—dc23

CONTENTS

FIGURES

Introduction

On Common Ground

John Emmeus Davis, Line Algoed,
and María E. Hernández-Torrales

When community land trusts (CLTs) began appearing in the United States during the 1970s, all of them were located in rural areas. Most were constructed along lines laid down in the first book to describe this "new model for land tenure in America" published in 1972,[1] which had based much of its own conception of a CLT on New Communities Inc., a cooperative farm founded in rural Georgia three years before. In these early CLTs, community ownership of land by a nonprofit, nongovernmental organization was combined with individual ownership of newly built houses, offering lower-income people an opportunity to become homeowners. Many of these rural CLTs also made land available for farming, forestry, and other productive enterprises, providing lower-income people with a path toward economic independence.[2]

By the 1980s and 1990s, this innovative form of tenure was spreading into cities, suburbs, and towns. The concerns of this new generation of urban CLTs were somewhat different that those of their rural predecessors. Homeownership remained a priority for most of them, but other activities and applications got added to the mix: revitalizing the built environment in distressed neighborhoods; preventing the displacement of low-income residents in gentrifying neighborhoods; and developing multiple types and tenures of permanently affordable housing, going beyond the detached, single-family, owner-occupied houses that were the programmatic focus of CLTs in more rural areas. The housing constructed (or rehabilitated) by CLTs in cities included townhouses, condominiums, limited-equity cooperatives, multi-family rentals, rooming houses, and facilities for the homeless. Some urban CLTs started going beyond housing as well, developing non-residential buildings for stores, restaurants, clinics, community centers, or facilities for other nonprofit organizations providing various goods and services for neighborhood residents. A few CLTs made vacant lots and larger parcels of land available for activities that evoked the model's rural pedigree, including greenhouses, community gardens, and small-scale commercial agriculture.

Today, a majority of community land trusts throughout the world are urban. Although CLTs are still being organized and operated in rural villages and towns, especially in England, the greatest growth in the global CLT movement has been occurring in the residential neighborhoods and inner-ring suburbs of cities—small, medium, and large. Most of this growth has happened in the Global North in cities like Boston, Brussels, Denver, London, Montreal, Oakland, and Toronto. More recently, however, urban CLTs have been appearing in the Global South as well, inspired in part by the *Fideicomiso de la Tierra del Caño Martín Peña* in San Juan, Puerto Rico. This urban CLT, after years of community-based organizing and planning, gained title to multiple parcels of publicly owned land underneath seven densely populated informal settlements along a tidal channel in the city's midst. As a result, the homes of 1500 families who had long lived precariously on lands they had not had a legal right to occupy were protected.

The work of the Caño Martín Peña CLT has caught the attention of community activists in other countries facing similar problems of land and housing insecurity. Brazil is a prime example. In Rio de Janeiro alone, 1.4 million people reside in a thousand informal settlements known as *favelas*. Several years ago, a network of leaders from several of Rio's favelas, supported by an NGO named Catalytic Communities, learned of the Caño CLT. They began exploring whether a CLT might be applied to regularizing land tenure beneath a favela's built environment. They invited representatives from the Caño CLT to visit Rio and offer advice on how they might organize CLTs of their own. This was the start of a formative, participatory planning process that is still unfolding.

Urbanists at the United Nations have also taken note of CLTs. At the 2016 UN Conference on Housing and Sustainable Urban Development in Quito, Ecuador, community land trusts were among the "policies, tools, mechanisms, and financing models" named in the *New Urban Agenda* for promoting access to housing and for making cities more inclusive. CLTs were touted as one of several "cooperative solutions" for addressing, in the *Agenda's* words, "the evolving needs of persons and communities, in order to improve the supply of housing, especially for low-income groups, prevent segregation, and [prevent] arbitrary forced evictions and displacements…with special attention to programmes for upgrading slums and informal settlements."[3]

Most urban CLTs do, in fact, have a programmatic focus on promoting and preserving access to housing, "especially for low-income groups." And many give special attention to addressing the needs of people at risk of being displaced, either because they are residing on lands for which they do not hold formal title or because they are being priced out of areas where land values and housing costs are rapidly rising.

This puts the emerging CLT movement at the intersection of two world-wide movements for social change. The first is occurring in countries where people who are land-insecure are struggling to gain recognition, registration, and legal protection for acreage that is occupied under some form of informal landholding system.[4] As in San Juan and Rio, not all of this land is rural. Many informal settlements are to be found in major and minor cities in Latin America, Asia, and Africa.

CLTs are also aligned with a rising tide of advocacy and action around housing rights that is evident in cities around the world. The issues being championed by this amorphous movement for a "right to the city" include rent control, community-led development, and the production and preservation of housing that remains permanently affordable. Popular support for CLTs and similar forms of community-controlled land and housing is surfacing amidst ongoing battles to prevent the displacement of classes and races at constant risk of being pushed aside by government investment in major infrastructure or private investment in upscale development. Such risks become especially acute—and protective interventions like a CLT become especially attractive—during periods of economic disruption when "disaster capitalists" lurk in the wings, waiting for any chance to buy up homes lost to foreclosure or to buy up lands cleared by wildfires, hurricanes, or floods.

Urban problems like these provided the backdrop for a collection of original essays published by Terra Nostra Press in June 2020, entitled *On Common Ground: International Perspectives on the Community Land Trust*. Many of the book's twenty-six chapters featured stories of CLTs in cities, where the CLT's distinctive approach to ownership, organization, and operation is being applied in urban neighborhoods. Eight of these chapters were selected for the present monograph.

It should be noted that all of the contributors to *On Common Ground* had finished writing their essays before the onset of the 2020 coronavirus pandemic, the consequent contraction of many national economies, and the reawakening of resistance to systemic racism. These momentous events, which have shaken cities to the core, have rendered irrelevant many of the conventional mechanisms used in the past by community organizers, city planners, nongovernmental organizations, and elected officials to promote affordable housing and neighborhood revitalization. That has not happened in the case of community-led development on community-owned land, however, the strategy employed by CLTs. Indeed, the stories told in the present monograph are evidence of the strategy's continuing effectiveness in meeting a host of urban challenges.

WHAT'S IN A NAME?

Community land trusts are not all alike. Among the hundreds of CLTs that already exist or are presently being planned, there are numerous variations in how these organizations are structured, how their lands are utilized, how development is done, and how the stewardship of housing is operationalized. What is called a "community land trust" can vary greatly from one country to another, even from one community to another within the same country.

The main features of the modern-day CLT were outlined in the seminal book published in 1972.[5] The book's authors based their blueprint on the experiment then underway at New Communities Inc., but they also drew on a number of historical precedents. These included the collectively owned lands of indigenous peoples, the town commons of New England, the *moshav ovdim* of Israel, the *ejidos* of Mexico, the *Ujamaa Vijijini* of Tanzania, and the *Gramdan* villages of India.[6]

The CLT model described in 1972 also resembled the mixed-ownership scheme that Ebenezer Howard had proposed in 1898 for his Garden Cities in England.[7] The houses, stores, orchards, and factories in the new towns he proposed to establish on the outskirts of major cities would be privately owned by individuals, cooperatives, or for-profit businesses, but the underlying land would be owned forever by a nongovernmental organization, created expressly for that purpose. These scattered parcels of land would then be made available for planned development and productive use through long-term ground leases, executed between the nonprofit landowner and myriad individuals who owned buildings or operated enterprises on the leaseholds. Land was to be held and managed on behalf of *all* residents—rich and poor, present and future—enabling a community to direct its own development, to determine its own fate, and to capture for the common good a majority of the gains in land value that society as a whole had helped to create.

To the mixed-ownership model pioneered in England, India, and elsewhere, the founders of New Communities—and the reflective practitioners who followed in their wake—added organizational and operational features of their own, turning the model into something different, something new. Community-owned land remained the foundation on which a CLT was to be established, with a private, nonprofit corporation holding and managing scattered parcels of land for the benefit of residents of a particular locale, especially low-income families in need of housing. What got *added* were mechanisms for ensuring that the development done by a CLT would be guided by the community, as would the organization itself. This was not development from above, dictated by a governmental body, a charitable investor, or a benevolent provider of social housing. It was development from below, directed by residents of the community a CLT had been organized to serve. Ownership and empowerment went hand-in-hand.[8]

Added, too, was an operational commitment to the stewardship of any lands entrusted to the CLT and of any buildings erected on its lands, most of which would be owned by somebody else. Projects pursued by a CLT were designed to ensure that housing, nonresidential buildings, and other land uses would remain continuously affordable, long after development was done.[9]

These distinctive features of ownership, organization, and operation, overlapping and interacting in a dynamic model of place-based development, became eventually known as the "classic" CLT. Almost as soon as nearly everyone came to agree on this particular conception and configuration of the community land trust, however, the model be-

COMMUNITY
(Organization)

LAND
(Ownership)

TRUST
(Operation)

gan to be modified in countless ways. Variations arose in every feature of the "classic" CLT, as practitioners in different places adapted it to fit conditions, needs, and priorities in their own communities or to fit customs and laws in their own countries.

This continuing process of innovation and adaptation has helped the CLT to spread across a disparate international landscape and to thrive in a range of settings. At the same time, the diversity of meanings attached to the model and the variety of ways in which CLTs are structured has introduced a degree of difficulty to the task of explaining exactly what a CLT might be. Today, there is ambiguity—even a dose of controversy—to be found in the description and implementation of every component.

Community. Throughout the world, most organizations that call themselves a CLT are committed to involving a place-based population in their activities, incorporating a participatory ethos into their organization's purposes, practices, and structure. People who live on the CLT's lands and those who live nearby are encouraged to become voting members of the organization. They are recruited to serve on its governing board.[10] They are invited to participate in shaping the uses and projects proposed by the CLT. Development is "community-led," along with the organization that initiates and oversees that development.

Ambiguity enters the picture because of the varying arrangements that CLTs employ in striving to engage and to empower their community. Controversy arises because some CLTs have dispensed with community altogether, causing critics to question whether they should even be considered a "real" CLT. The traditional model's distinctive features of ownership and operation might be present, but residents who are served by the program neither govern nor guide it; that is, "community" is missing from the organizational make-up of the entity doing development. Variations like these create perennial challenges for CLT advocates whenever they try to reach a consensus as to what deserves to be deemed a "community land trust."[11]

Land. The typical CLT is a nonprofit organization that removes land permanently from the marketplace, managing it on behalf of a place-based community while making it available for long-term use by individuals and organizations. Title to the buildings on a CLTs land, either those existing when the CLT acquired the land or those constructed later on, is held individually by any number of parties—homeowners, cooperatives, businesses, gardeners, farmers, etc. The underlying land is leased from the CLT by the buildings' owners.

This mixed-ownership arrangement blurs the legal and conceptual boundary between conventional categories of tenure, where real property is presumed to be one thing or the other. A community land trust messes up this tidy picture, for it is balanced half-way between the two extremes of *individual property*, owned and operated primarily for the purpose of promoting private interests; and *collective property*, owned and operated to promote a common interest. The CLT tilts toward the former in its treatment of buildings. It tilts toward the latter in its treatment of land, making the CLT a first cousin to cooperatives, co-housing, and various forms of communal, collective, and tribal land.

Although a CLT's lands are frequently and fairly characterized as "community-owned" or, in the parlance of the present volume, as "common ground," these landholdings are neither collectively nor cooperatively owned by the people living on them or around them. Title is held exclusively by the CLT. A community land trust is ownership for the common good, not ownership in common.[12]

There are places, however, where the separation of ownership is made difficult (or impossible) by quirks in the property laws of a particular country or by the quibbles of prospective funders. CLTs have sometimes been compelled, therefore, to retain ownership of buildings as well as the land or to relinquish ownership of both, while imposing long-lasting restrictions on the use and affordability of these properties. Another variation has been developed in Puerto Rico, where the Caño Martín Peña CLT holds the underlying land but uses a durable surface rights deed, rather than a ground lease, to provide security of tenure for people who own and occupy houses on the CLT's land. Some of these residents are living on sites their families have occupied for nearly a hundred years.

Trust. Although "trust" is part of their given name, CLTs have rarely been established as real estate trusts.[13] Most are NGOs—private, nonprofit corporations with a charitable purpose of meeting the needs of populations who are regularly underserved by both the market and the state. "Trust" refers not to how a CLT is organized, but to how it is operated. "Trust" is what a CLT *does* in overseeing the lands and buildings under its care and in performing the duties of stewardship. Foremost among these duties is the preservation of affordability, ensuring long-term access to land and housing for people of modest means and preventing their displacement due to gentrification and other pressures. Stewardship also includes such responsibilities as preventing deferred maintenance in housing and other buildings on the CLT's land and intervening, if necessary, to protect occupants against predatory lending, arbitrary eviction, mortgage foreclosure, and other threats to security of tenure. Some CLTs are focused less on the provision of housing, however, than on the preservation of watersheds, woodlands, or agricultural lands, either in rural or urban areas. The responsibilities of a CLT entrusted with managing such lands can look very different than the stewardship needed when affordable housing is a CLT's operational focus.

WHAT'S SHARED IN COMMON?

Despite this lack of uniformity in the description, implementation, and application of CLTs, there are commonalities nonetheless. What unites a global community of CLT scholars and practitioners is more important than what separates us. There is a *lingua franca* for understanding what it means for an organization to be a CLT and to behave like one. There is a shared commitment to reinventing and repurposing real estate for the common good. There is a shared conviction that community-owned land, in particular, is likely to do a better job of promoting equitable and sustainable development than land that is commodified and owned individually, especially in places populated by groups that have long been disadvantaged and disempowered.

Another trait that is shared by most CLT scholars and practitioners is a conviction that the whole of a CLT is greater than the sum of its parts. Across the diverse landscape of CLTs, ownership, organization, and operation are not configured exactly the same in every town and country. Wherever this strategy has been adopted, however, there is a general recognition that it takes more than a single component to make a CLT; it takes more than the reinvention of any one of them to bend the arc of development toward a fairer distribution of property and power. Community-owned land, by itself, is not enough. Community-led development is not enough. Permanently affordable housing is not enough. It is their *combination* that gives a CLT its distinctive identity and transformative potential.[14]

To be sure, there are places in the world where CLTs have been effective without adopting every feature of the "classic" CLT. That model is no longer a template, but it remains a touchstone. It is where most people start, when striving to adapt this complex form of tenure to their own situations. It is where most people hope a CLT will lead, when envisioning a better outcome from their arduous, virtuous labors, whether providing affordable housing, rebuilding residential neighborhoods, regularizing tenure in informal settlements, or preserving productive lands and local enterprises at risk of being lost to market pressures.

When land is owned for the common good of a place-based community, present and future; when development is done by an organization that is a creature of that community, rooted in it, accountable to it, and guided by it; when stewardship is deliberate, diligent, and durable . . . justice is more likely to be achieved. And more likely to last. That is the moral impetus and lofty promise of common ground.

Notes

1. International Independence Institute, *The Community Land Trust: A Guide to a New Model for Land Tenure in America* (Cambridge MA: Center for Community Economic Development, 1972).

2. Mtamanika Youngblood, who had participated as a youth in the early efforts to establish New Communities Inc., was interviewed many years later for a documentary about this pioneering CLT (*Arc of Justice: The Rise, Fall and Rebirth of a Beloved Community,* Open Studio Productions, 2016). On camera, she described the multiple purposes of this rural initiative: "The idea behind New Communities was to take civil rights one step further into economic independence and economic rights, using agriculture as an economic base."

3. United Nations. *New Urban Agenda.* Adopted at the Conference on Housing and Sustainable Urban Development (Habitat III) in Quito, Ecuador, on 20 October 2016 and endorsed by the United Nations General Assembly at its sixty-eighth plenary meeting of the seventy-first session on 23 December 2016. (Paragraph 107 appears on page 27.) Available at: *http://habitat3.org/the-new-urban-agenda/*

4. Depending on the country, such property is termed communal, collective, customary, native, indigenous, or community land. These terms for socially-based, collective land-holding are borrowed from Liz Alden Wily, "Challenges for the New Kid on the Block — Collective Property," Chapter 5 in *On Common Ground: International Per-spectives on the Community Land Trust* (Madison WI: Terra Nostra Press, 2020).

5. International Independence Institute (1972), op. cit.

6. Other intellectual influences and historical precedents acknowledged by the book's authors included Henry George, Ralph Borsodi, Mildrid Loomis, and the planned, leased-land communities of Bryn Gweled Homesteads near Philadelphia and Morning-side Gardens outside of New York City. More information on the ideas and exper-iments that gave rise to the CLT can be found in "Origins and Evolution of the Community Land Trust in the United States," Pp. 3-47 in J.E. Davis (ed.) *The Community Land Trust Reader* (Cambridge MA: Lincoln Institute of Land Policy, 2010); and in "Les Philos-ophes de Terrain et Les Pionniers," Pp. 19-44 in *Manuel d'antispeculation immobiliere* (Montreal, Quebec: Les Editions Ecosociete, 2014).

7. Ebenezer Howard, Garden Cities of To-Morrow (Swan Sonnenshein & Co., 1902).

8. This interweaving of ownership and empowerment was never far from the minds of the African-Americans who pioneered the first CLT. A brochure for New Communities, Inc., printed in the 1970s, described the purpose of a land trust in this way: "It is people holding land together as a community; it is 'people power,' the security of holding and owning together the land which, through development and use, will bring them the

power to stand on their own two feet."

9. This is achieved through the CLT's ownership of the underlying land and its imposition of contractual controls over the buildings' rents and resales. Aside from determining how the land is to be used, these contractual con-trols — typically imposed through a 99-year ground lease — regulate the occupancy, upkeep, improvement, financing, behest, and resale of any buildings sited on the CLT's land.

10. Organizationally, the model promoted by the Institute for Community Economics during the 1980s had an open membership and a three-part board, representing the interests of the people who live on the CLT's land, people who live within the CLT's service area, and institutions that served that geography, including government, churches, banks, businesses, and other NGOs. See Institute for Community Economics, *The Community Land Trust Hand-book* (Emmaus PA: Rodale Press, 1982).

11. To a certain degree, we sidestepped this definitional debate in *On Common Ground* (2020) by featuring among the book's twenty-six chapters a number of organizations that *self-identify* as a community land trust, even if they do not exhibit every feature of what is known in the USA as the "classic" CLT. Our ecumenical embrace had limits, however. We admitted to the company of CLTs only organizations that were committed to removing land per-manently from the stream of commerce, placing it under the ownership or control of a designated community and stewarding that land for the common good.

12. This echoes the earliest description of the CLT: "The community land trust is not primarily concerned with common ownership. Rather, its concern is ownership for the common good, which may or may not be combined with common ownership." International Independence Institute (1972), op cit., page 1. Although the people living on a CLT's land do not hold title to the underlying land, the resale formula used by some CLTs does provide for a modest increase in the homeowner's equity if the land has appreciated in value during the homeowner's tenure.

13. Trusts are established by individuals to control the distribution of their property, either during their lifetimes or after their death. Property is often real estate, but it may also be stocks, bonds, or other income-generating as-sets. The person who creates the trust is called the "settlor." The person who holds the property for another's behalf is the "trustee." The latter takes title to the property, although under a "revocable trust" the settlor may later reclaim ownership. Proceeds from the trust are distributed by the trustee to a specific list of beneficiaries named by the settlor when the trust was established.

14. An argument for CLTs being more than the sum of their parts can be found in John Emmeus Davis, "Better Together: The Challenging, Transformative Complexity of Community, Land, and Trust," Chapter 26 in *On Common Ground* (2020), op cit.

1.

Making a Case for CLTs in All Markets, Even Cold Ones

Steve King

The Community Land Trust is a proven tool
for change. When shall we dare use it?[1]
— *Susan Witt and Robert Swann*

Over the past several decades in the United States, there has been a resurgent interest in a certain quality of life afforded by dense urban living, particularly among well-educated, high-income earners. This has precipitated a re-segregation of the population in hot-market metropolitan areas like the one surrounding San Francisco, where housing production has failed to keep pace with economic growth. The persistent, racialized disinvestment and neglect that for decades targeted sections of the Bay Area, including East and West Oakland, Bayview Hunters Point, East Palo Alto, and Richmond, has nearly vanished, as real estate speculators have found opportunities to buy up land and buildings in proximity to downtown San Francisco and Silicon Valley. Long-time working-class residents have been steadily pushed to far-flung exurbs in search of affordability, at the expense of social networks, increased commute times, and diminished cultural connection. Many who remain in the inner Bay Area have been subjected to adverse housing-related by-products of the booming economy, including skyrocketing rents, involuntary displacement, no-fault evictions, tent encampments, and a near paralysis among public officials over how to ameliorate the resulting harm.

This predicament is not unique to the Bay Area, and it is also not shared uniformly across the United States. At the other end of the economic spectrum, many older industrial towns, cities, and regions have experienced a seemingly irreversible downward spiral marked by a long decline of the manufacturing sector, a shrinking middle class, white flight and suburbanization, and the recent foreclosure crisis. Many places that once flourished around specific industries are struggling to survive in the absence of the economic

> We are still lacking a broader argument for why CLTs might be effective in places that are plagued by disinvestment, not reinvestment.

engines that once powered them. Abandonment, high vacancy rates, plummeting home values, municipal fiscal crises, and extreme poverty are but a few of the challenges left in the wake of economic decline. For people living in such cold-market neighborhoods or cities, the prospect of gentrification seems remote, a distant threat that is unlikely ever to materialize.

Urban growth and decline are both uneven and cyclical. If there is one constant about cities in an advanced capitalist economy, it is that they change over time. Indeed, these antipodal cases mask the middling nuances of urban development in post-Industrial American cities. As the urban planner Alan Mallach has noted, even in shrinking, "divided" cities like Detroit, Cleveland, and St. Louis, the investment in high-end, amenity-rich housing is an emergent phenomenon; just a few blocks away from new, upscale development there remains relentless neighborhood decline and poverty.[2]

In hot-market coastal cities and in cold-market metro areas alike, therefore, economic opportunity is not equitably distributed. The benefits of development overwhelmingly accrue to the wealthy, while the burdens disproportionately impact the poor. A similar pattern is found in housing and land use. History is replete with examples of how both public policies and private actions have been divisive, exclusionary, predatory, and destructive, especially for African-American neighborhoods and other communities of color.

Fig. 1.1. Weak-market neighborhood, Old North St. Louis, Missouri, 2014.

A premise and promise of the community land trust model is that it aims straight for the heart of a major cause of these persistent inequities: the ownership and control of land. The fundamental desires for freedom, self-determination, and rootedness *in place* were core motivations for the creation of the first modern CLT in Albany, Georgia nearly fifty years ago. And they remain so today, which is a reason why CLTs are increasingly utilized in neighborhoods and cities with ascending real estate markets. Community activists — and some public officials — see in the CLT a strategic tool to counter the negative externalities of market-driven development that are inflicted disproportionately on low-income households and communities of color. A forceful rhetorical case has been made — and some empirical evidence is beginning to appear — demonstrating that community control of land via a CLT can be an effective hedge against market forces that otherwise displace precariously housed people in disempowered neighborhoods.[3] The development of CLTs in cities like Seattle, Portland, San Francisco, Los Angeles, Denver, Austin, Houston, Washington, DC, Boston, and New York City attests to the allure and applicability of CLTs in ascending markets.

In contrast — and strangely so — a compelling case has never been made for CLTs in cold-market locales, despite the fact that a number of CLTs have succeeded in places where real estate markets are weak.[4] John Emmeus Davis has offered a cogent argument that "counter-cyclical stewardship," the particular forte of CLTs, can be a stabilizing force amidst market fluctuations.[5] We also have some evidence of CLTs bearing out this promise of stability in market troughs, as happened during the foreclosure crisis of 2008–2012 when CLT homeowners did not lose their homes.[6] Nevertheless, we are still lacking a broader argument for why CLTs might be effective in places that are plagued by disinvestment, not reinvestment; that is, places where affordability is not the most pressing issue and where market-instigated displacement is not an imminent threat. This essay is an initial attempt to fill this void, offering a rationale and a provisional menu of strategic options for community control of land via a CLT in cold-market areas.

CHALLENGES AND OPPORTUNITES FOR CLT DEVELOPMENT IN COLD MARKETS

There is a widespread belief amongst practitioners, funders, and institutions in the broader community development and affordable housing fields that the CLT model is neither needed nor workable in cold real estate markets. This reductive conclusion belies an unfortunate misunderstanding of the goals and values of many emerging (and established) CLTs. It is a potentially destructive preconception that can stifle support of new CLT initiatives and thwart important community-driven work before it is given a chance to thrive. Before delving squarely into the qualities of cold-market places and the potential for CLTs in those areas, therefore, it is necessary to consider briefly the question of the relationship between the "strength" of a local real estate market (hot/strong vs. lukewarm/moderate vs. cold/weak) and the prospects for creating a viable CLT.

CLTs operate in a manner that works to correct for defects in both the private market and the broader political system, producing equitable and sustainable outcomes that would not otherwise emerge from either. This ameliorative impact can occur in *any* market. In this respect, the market itself is a precondition for a CLT. If a more just and democratic system was in place that equitably distributed land, housing, and economic opportunity, a CLT might not be needed. In the absence of such a system, however, there is a redistributive and reparative role for CLTs to play, regardless of the relative strength of the local economy and local real estate market.

The feasibility and viability of a CLT in any market — including cold ones — will depend on a complex array of local conditions and factors, including: the type of activities a community is hoping a CLT will undertake; who is invited to (or excluded from) a CLT's decision-making table; and, perhaps most importantly, the presence (or absence) of residents who have organized to improve their neighborhood and to secure a more just allocation of resources. Each of these contingencies offers a window into why a CLT might be the ideal vehicle for equitable development in a cold market.

Cold-market challenges. What are some of the conditions and challenges for doing community development in cold-market areas? By its very nature, a cold-market city or neighborhood suffers from a lack of investment and has relatively little economic activity. Within these geographies, economic opportunity for low-income residents is typically scarce and may lead to declining or unstable populations. The relative lack of private economic activity is often matched, moreover, by limited public investment in services and infrastructure.

> Just because property values have declined in a cold market does not mean that housing tenure is secure.

Spillover effects of a depressed economy are reflected in the built environment. Elevated vacancy levels are a common attribute of cold markets, including both unoccupied or abandoned buildings and vacant or undeveloped land. When vacancy levels climb, the condition and value of the overall building stock begins to deteriorate. Declining property values attract unscrupulous speculators looking to drain the remaining value at the further expense of the building stock and to the detriment of existing residents. This speculative activity is frequently carried out by absentee owners — investors with no connection to the community and no qualms about extracting wealth from struggling residents and their neighborhoods. These conditions invariably put a strain on local government, as property tax revenues wither and the requisite finances for public services begin to evaporate. Public education, infrastructure, public works, parks, and other public facilities — the basic building blocks of civic life — can languish as a result of diminished municipal revenues. Thus begins a vicious, self-reinforcing web of disinvestment and deterioration that is difficult to arrest.

Just because property values have declined in a cold market does not mean that housing tenure is secure. Nor does it mean that housing quality is safe and healthy or that rents are affordable relative to wages. Evictions occur across the entire strong-market/weak-market continuum in the United States, with especially high concentrations in many cold-market areas of the American South, and disproportionate impacts for low-income, African-American, and female-headed households.[7]

While low-income renters are the most vulnerable in this regard, market-rate homeownership is not necessarily more secure. One indication is the ten million home foreclosures that occurred during the Great Recession, beginning in 2008. Another indication is the enormous number of "severely cost-burdened" homeowners in the United States who earn below the median income for their area and pay more than half their income for housing. In cold-market areas, homeownership might be relatively more affordable for households of modest means, compared to hot-market cities, but it may still be out of reach because wages have stagnated amidst a distressed economy. Moreover, for households who do manage to buy a home in cold-market places, the quality of that housing may be low, especially at the bottom end of the market. And for cost-burdened homeowners, there is usually little money left after paying their monthly housing bills to keep up with necessary repairs.

For residents living in areas where these types of conditions exist, there can be deep physical and psychological trauma, as well as other health-negating influences, including a lack of access to essential services and healthy food options, limited opportunities for sufficient and meaningful work, fractured networks of social capital, poor housing conditions, and overall neighborhood distress. All are fundamental determinants of health and well-being. All tend to deteriorate in a cold-market city or neighborhood where opportunity is restricted.

Cold-market assets. Despite the compounding negative conditions facing residents of cold-market cities and neighborhoods, these places are also replete with many positive and potentially productive assets. The challenge is how to utilize and to leverage those assets in a context of scarcity. Conditions will vary from one place to another, but there are four key assets that may form the basis for CLT development in cold-market areas.

First, land may be plentiful and relatively inexpensive. This is typically one of the most significant barriers to CLT expansion in hot-market areas. By contrast, in cold markets, land that is undeveloped, underutilized, or vacant is often more plentiful — and potentially less costly.

Second, the market demand for buildings (along with land) of any type (residential, commercial, industrial, etc.) is likely suppressed, which may be accompanied by deteriorated physical conditions, tax delinquency, or functional obsolescence. These are not insignificant challenges in terms of liability and the resources needed for acquisition,

Fig. 1.2. Resident leaders of the East 12th Street Coalition, Oakland, California, demanding community involvement in planning for the redevelopment of land.

rehabilitation, or even demolition, yet a building stock with limited demand and a low cost may still provide an opportunity for CLT development.

Third, people with roots in any place-based community are its most valuable asset. Long-time residents, newcomers, children, families, elders, the displaced, and the house-less — all form the potential base of people-power, waiting to be engaged, to lead, and to craft new solutions to old problems.[8]

Finally, most cold-market places already have a set of community development entities, nonprofit organizations, and faith-based institutions working in and among the community, providing social services and tackling many of the problems noted above. These groups can be sources of financial, technical, and political support for a new CLT. In some cases, a preexisting organization may even take the lead in initiating a CLT or choose to house a fledgling CLT under its corporate umbrella.[9]

These place-based assets provide the opportunity to think expansively about the value and possibilities of the CLT model in areas where the economic rationale around permanent affordability — the most frequently touted benefit of CLTs — is less than compelling due to prevailing market conditions. If the looming loss of housing affordability as a market feature is not a pressing issue, however, then why else might a community want to consider creation of a CLT? Some strategic possibilities are considered below.

BEYOND HOMEOWNERSHIP: EXPLORING THE MYRIAD OPTIONS FOR COMMUNITY-OWNED LAND IN COLD MARKETS

One of the most powerful attributes of the CLT model is its versatility; it is deployable across a range of land uses and societal needs, as identified by its community. Yet, this broad applicability has been underutilized as CLTs have grown in popularity for a primary use: affordable housing in general, and owner-occupied housing in particular.

> Community-led development on community-owned land is the essence of a CLT.

The scant attention paid to CLT development in cold-market areas, therefore, may derive in part from the manner in which the field has advanced over the past several decades. CLTs have become largely synonymous with the production and stewardship of *permanently affordable homeownership*. This is undoubtedly an important and laudable achievement. But narrowing the model's focus to a single purpose has resulted in minimizing the importance of a more fundamental building block: community-owned and community-governed land. Indeed, it can be argued that community-led development on community-owned land is the essence of a CLT, rather than the permanent affordability of owner-occupied housing. The former is *the* feature that connects the CLT of today to the founders of New Communities, Inc. and their struggle for justice, liberation, and self-determination.[10]

The framework of community-led development on community-owned land forms the basis for considering the strategic potential of CLTs in cold-market areas. It provides an opening to explore nascent possibilities for project development and collective action that are currently under-examined and undervalued in the burgeoning CLT field, at least in the United States. Beyond permanently affordable homeownership, the range of opportunity for CLTs is extensive. Many housing-oriented CLTs have, in fact, already expanded their purviews to include projects with non-residential land uses, with affiliated or mission-supporting lines of business. A cursory look at some of these expansive uses and creative possibilities will help to demonstrate the potential for community-owned land in cold-market areas.

Community Gardens, Sustainable Agriculture, and Open Space

One of the most common non-residential uses of CLT land has been for food production. This option may be particularly relevant in low-income, cold-market neighborhoods where access to fresh and healthy food is often limited. There are plentiful examples of existing CLTs that steward land for growing food and food-related businesses.[11] These range from small infill community gardens to multi-acre farms and large-scale open space and agricultural land conservation. In cold-market areas where vacant land may be relatively accessible (either via fee simple ownership or long-term leasing arrangements managed by a CLT), small-scale urban agriculture or community gardening can serve as a catalytic starting point for new organizations that may not yet have the capacity or resources to undertake larger or costlier real estate projects. Additionally, the activation of an underutilized or problematic parcel with neighborhood residents and partners can serve as a powerful community-building and organizing vehicle to develop goodwill, awareness, and support for additional activities on community-owned land.

As one example, the first property acquired by the Parkdale Neighbourhood Land Trust (PNLT) in Toronto, Canada was a site for gardening, and has served as a successful precursor to other CLT acquisitions. In 2017, PNLT acquired the 7,000 square-foot Milky Way Garden parcel to be permanently preserved as a community-controlled asset. The site plays a particularly vital role for newcomers from Tibet to build community and to grow culturally-appropriate produce. The campaign to acquire the lot also played a galvanizing role to raise funds from community residents and to bolster awareness of the mission of the CLT. PNLT owns the lot and is active in facilitating the community vision for the parcel, leasing the land to a partner organization to manage on a day-to-day basis.

On a much larger scale, the Athens Land Trust (ALT) in Athens, Georgia has established an impressive program of land conservation and community agriculture in addition to their affordable housing work. As of 2017, the Athens Land Trust had protected 16,485 acres of land in 36 Georgia counties via both conservation easements and ownership. These holdings included "natural habitats and river frontage, working agricultural land and land of historical significance, and land for public recreation."[12] Additionally, ALT's vibrant community agricultural program provides much-needed access to land — as well as programmatic support — for growing food and food-related businesses. As a steward of land across a diverse range of uses, ALT utilizes these assets to create programs

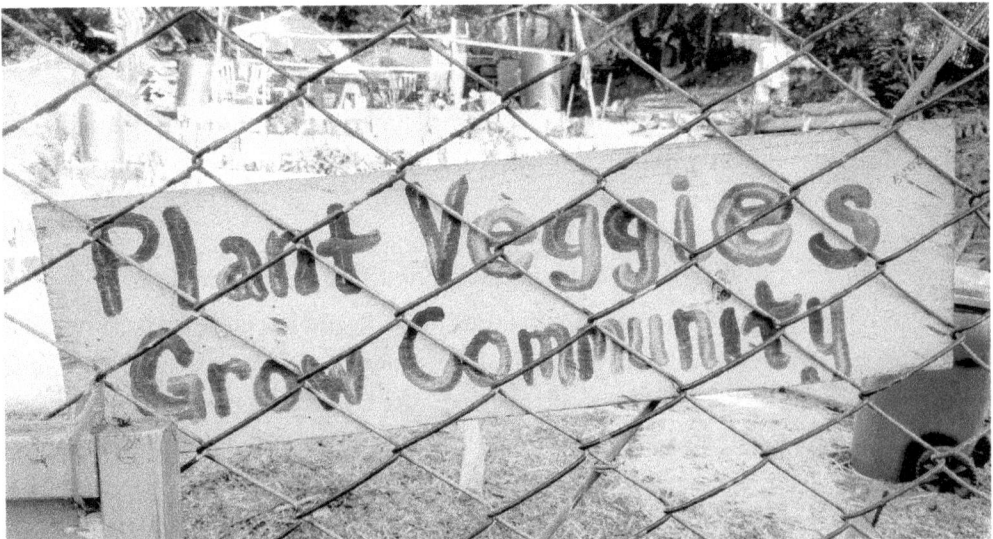

Fig. 1.3. Community garden, Oakland, California.

offering paid career development and training opportunities for young people in the construction trades, urban farming, and land conservation—all with an eye toward nurturing future generations of local leadership around land-based justice and opportunity.

Commercial Land Uses

Commercial uses for community-owned land span an incredibly diverse mix of options and scales. The possibilities are endless, limited only by what a community can envision and by what a municipality will permit according to its zoning and building codes. In the commercial context, as with other CLT land tenure arrangements, a CLT can play the foundational role of acquiring land and leasing it out to support community-prioritized economic development, or the CLT can own and manage both the land and the improvements.[13] Existing commercial CLT uses include not only stewarding land and buildings for mission-aligned nonprofit and community-serving organizations, but also for more unusual uses such as a gas station in a rural California coastal community (the Bolinas CLT's Bo-Gas) and a mobile meat-processing facility in rural Washington State (Lopez CLT).

In cold-market areas, a CLT might play a particularly valuable role in supporting non-residential strategies that produce targeted economic benefits and job opportunities for residents who have been harmed by disinvestment. To cite an example from another country, the Homebaked CLT in Liverpool, England got started in 2012 as a reaction to a top-down, government-initiated urban renewal plan to demolish a swath of historic buildings in the neighborhood of Anfield.[14] In response, residents coalesced around a vision to save a cherished neighborhood bakery, turning it into a cooperatively owned business. The Homebaked CLT was established to acquire the bakery building and to implement a community-led vision for redeveloping the neighborhood's commercial district. Saving the bakery served as the catalyzing project by: initiating the CLT; preserving a visible anchor business; and laying the groundwork for a more expansive agenda for community-owned land in the neighborhood.

Back in the USA, the Lopez CLT in Washington State serves as the steward for a number of commercial storefronts that provide incubator space for small, local businesses. All twelve of the businesses that utilize these spaces are owned by homeowner-leaseholders of the Lopez CLT. Connecting economic and housing security, these commercial spaces offer CLT residents an opportunity to build individual assets in ways that do not put their homes at risk, while generating local economic benefits that circulate within the community.

Subsidiary, Affiliated, and Mutually-Supporting Businesses

Across the national landscape, there are more and more cases of CLTs creating affiliated entities or businesses that either bolster the work of the CLT or create aligned opportunities for CLT residents and members. For instance, both Proud Ground, a CLT in

Portland, Oregon, and the Northern California Land Trust in Berkeley, California have established real estate brokerages to support in-house property transactions and to generate revenue for the CLT through non-CLT transactions. One Roof Community Housing, a CLT in Duluth, Minnesota has set up a subsidiary firm to do construction and home rehabilitation for the parent organization. In Berkeley and Oakland, California, three CLTs have come together to explore the creation of a worker-owned property management cooperative to support the needs of resident-operated CLT properties, housing cooperatives, worker cooperatives, and other aligned organizations. It is envisioned that the property management cooperative will leverage the skills of existing CLT residents and co-op worker-owners to provide basic property management services as well as capacity building among a broad network of allied organizations.

CLT as Steward and Supporter of Community Health and Stability

As John Emmeus Davis has reminded us, the stewardship function of a CLT is not just about maintaining affordability — it also includes the preservation of housing *quality* and *security*.[15] Even in markets where affordability may not be a pressing concern, there are important roles a CLT can play in supporting residents with maintenance, repair, and overall housing quality, as well as intervening to cure defaults, advocating for better public policies and services with and for CLT homeowners and tenants, and preventing displacement via foreclosure or eviction.

Some of these services may also be offered to non-CLT residents, particularly in areas where such services are lacking. Many existing CLTs, for example, already provide pre- and post-purchase homeowner education, credit counseling, and income and asset development coaching for anyone living within their service area, regardless of whether they are CLT homeowners. Depending upon what is needed in a community, a CLT might offer home repair and maintenance support, small business coaching and loans, tenant legal services, and various forms of renter, homebuyer, homeowner, and homelessness assistance.[16]

BEYOND DEVELOPMENT:
PLANNING, ORGANIZING, AND BUILDING POWER

In cold-market areas where housing affordability is not a priority issue, there may still be significant barriers to engagement, democratic participation, and decision-making related to intersecting economic, political, and ecological issues that disproportionately impact low-income residents and people of color. For these reasons, the resident-centered governance structure of a CLT can serve as a hub to meaningfully assess, analyze, and advance the needs of those struggling most severely in a cold market. Further, a CLT can be a potent vehicle for leadership development, resident organizing, and base-building as a precursor to actually pursuing community-led real estate activities.[17] Community organizing and base-building can, in turn, help to nurture the conditions in which a CLT emerges, grows, and thrives. An organized cohort of resident leaders and CLT members can hold elected officials accountable, exert political pressure when needed, and wield the people-power required to evidence a demand for community-led development on community-owned land.

The Dudley Street Neighborhood Initiative (DSNI) — and its affiliated CLT, Dudley Neighbors, Inc. (DNI) — in the Roxbury section of Boston provide instructive examples of community organizing and base-building in what was once a cold-market neighborhood. DNI is frequently touted as one of the most successful community land trusts in the United States, although few other CLTs have taken up their intentional model of broad-based resident empowerment and community-led planning and development. That approach to community development remains as audacious today as it was in 1984 when DSNI was founded.[18]

From the outset, DSNI was strategically oriented to support two core activities: place-based organizing of neighborhood residents and resident-led visioning and planning. When combined with the organization's affiliated community land trust, these activities comprised the productive inputs for enacting a community-building strategy on community-owned and community-controlled land.[19] This approach remains particularly vital because it puts the leadership of existing residents at the center of a strategy that builds

Fig. 1.4. Alliance of Californians for Community Empowerment. Oakland CLT homeowners, Shekinah Samaya-Thomas and Chris Thomas, join Vanessa Bulnes (with megaphone), advocating for resident-controlled housing on community-owned land.

upon both individual and community capacities and assets. In cities and neighborhoods where low-income residents and communities of color have been systematically disempowered and traumatized by market activity and public policy, this is a fundamental first step toward a restorative, just, and equitable redistribution of power. As Gus Newport, DSNI's former executive director, has observed:

> To successfully redevelop neighborhoods which have become blighted through years of neglect due to bank "redlining," failed government programs and poor planning, the only way that these areas can be turned around is with the will and involvement of concerned neighbors. A true foundation which will assure long term participation and neighborhood stabilization only happens when people can see and feel that their involvement and control (empowerment) is real. Anything short of this will result in additional failure, which is what we have in the majority of inner cities across the United States.[20]

BEYOND THE COLD-MARKET PRESENT: PLANNING FOR A JUST AND EQUITABLE FUTURE

Market Conditions Change: Safeguarding the Future

For people affiliated with CLTs in warm-market or hot-market areas, it is common to wistfully ponder an alternate reality in which the CLT might have emerged a decade or two earlier, when land and housing cost a fraction of current prices. By contrast, in cold-market areas, few people can imagine a future reality when costs will soar and a wave of investment and high-end development will threaten to displace low-income and moderate-income residents who are presently there. How can these two disparate perspectives be reconciled?

Equitable development is possible, but it must be coaxed into existence with political pressure and inclusive, democratic participation.

History serves as a guide on a specific point related to the failure of markets to provide for those most in need and the inability of political institutions to anticipate or to pre-emptively set the stage for truly equitable outcomes from development. Disinvestment has often been a precursor to new waves of private investment in stagnant real estate markets. The priority of government officials in such situations is often to incentivize *any* investment in housing or commercial development, rather than risk scaring investors away by requiring the benefits of development to be shared with residents who are most in need.

Equitable development is possible, but it must be coaxed into existence with political pressure and inclusive, democratic participation. This provides a basic rationale for building the infrastructure of a CLT in the absence of an imminent threat of displacement. Quite simply, local residents, who are often excluded from participating in development decisions, deserve a seat at the table. In many communities, the only way to assert this right is to organize, to build community power, to demand accountability, and to take control of development under the collective formation of a CLT.

There is also a need for a more nuanced understanding of the profound temporal balancing act in which CLTs are engaged. CLTs hold land for community benefit for a very long time. While CLTs and their members enact programs that address immediate resident-identified needs, CLTs must simultaneously uphold an extraordinary long-term vision for land reform and social justice. This delicate balance of community priorities across different timelines is a rarely acknowledged and woefully underappreciated hallmark of the CLT. In a cold market, the organizational container to hold land and to promote equitable development across a longer arc of time may reveal new avenues for pursuing community resilience and sustainability.

Markets Are the Problem:
Planning for a Future We Actually Want

Given the legacy and persistence of racial discrimination in housing and urban development and the disparate impact of development on specific populations, it is practical for a historically deprived and disempowered community to demand more control over the ownership, use, and development of land. In cold-market areas, in particular, it is both logical and strategic to pursue alternative solutions rather than the same top-down, market-reliant approaches that have harmed, disenfranchised, and marginalized communities in the past.

There is a growing cohort of community development organizers and practitioners who view the common stewardship of land as part of a fundamental bridge to an emancipatory future that will supplant the current market-based system. These explicitly visionary, transformational, and political efforts are ambitious roadmaps for a *just transition* to a more equitable, healthy, and sustainable future.[21]

Cooperation Jackson in Jackson, Mississippi provides an especially compelling example of a comprehensive project for sustainable, resident-led development, economic democracy, and community ownership. Jackson is a city that exhibits many features of a cold market. The organizers of Cooperation Jackson understand, however, that should the local economy eventually improve through market-based approaches, the needs of Jackson's black and brown residents are unlikely to be met.

Kali Akuno of Cooperation Jackson sees a strategic opportunity in the fact that Jackson's economy is presently depressed. It creates "breathing room" on the margins to envision and to enact a grand plan for a better, more just future. In his words:

> We harness this breathing room by exploiting the fact that there is minimal competition in the area to serve as a distraction or dilution of our focus, a tremendous degree of pent-up social demand waiting to be fulfilled and a deep reservoir of unrealized human potential waiting to be tapped.[22]

Along with a solidarity network of democratically-run, worker-owned cooperative enterprises, Cooperation Jackson has developed the Fannie Lou Hamer Community Land Trust as a core element of its long-term vision for developing and sustaining a new economic base for local residents. The importance of bringing more land into the CLT is one of long-term survival in the face of ongoing racial discrimination and economic austerity. As Akuno has said: "If the land shifts, the power shifts."[23]

Restoring Indigenous Land Stewardship

For those who come to the CLT in search of a model for land-based justice, many believe that the only way to achieve a truly just and equitable future will be to acknowledge and to repair the centuries of harm that have been inflicted upon indigenous peoples through colonial systems of enclosure, exclusion, and expropriation of tribal lands.

Fig. 1.5. Rammay Garden, Sogorea Te Land Trust, West Oakland, California, 2019.

Indigenous women leaders of the Sogorea Te Land Trust in Northern California provide one example. They are developing a new pathway to return ancestral Chochenyo and Karkin Ohlone lands to indigenous stewardship. Their vision is to restore sacred Ohlone land to a state that precedes and transcends the market-based system of private property. The leaders of the Sogorea Te Land Trust are seeding a transformative conversation that invites all residents of the Bay Area to reevaluate their relationship to the land they inhabit and to acknowledge that indigenous people co-inhabit their ancestral homelands alongside non-native residents, despite a contested history.

CLTs everywhere have an important role to play as allies in support of indigenous land struggles. In the particular context of cold markets, one potential avenue for advocacy resides in the re-conveyance of land that has been cheapened in terms of market logic, but may hold deep religious or cultural value for indigenous peoples.

In some cold-market neighborhoods, cities, and regions, a depressed economy with devalued real estate may present a unique opportunity, where a restorative conversation around returning land to indigenous stewardship could take root.

—

CONCLUSION

Even in stable markets with established CLTs, private and public support for community-led development on community-owned land often remains tenuous. The model has yet to gain the broad-based acceptance it deserves, despite the stellar performance of CLTs to date.[24] Given that many CLTs work exclusively in communities of color and that most CLT housing is developed for low-income households, the inequitable distribution of resources to support the development and expansion of affordable housing on CLT land must necessarily be viewed as a racial and economic justice issue. This is a reality affecting hot, cold, and lukewarm markets alike.

> The lack of resources being made available for the expansion of CLTs in the USA is due less to what a CLT is, than to who it benefits.

The lack of resources being made available for the expansion of CLTs in the USA is due less to what a CLT *is,* than to *who* it benefits. It is a reflection of how deeply entrenched the current system of housing delivery remains; how little room there is for models of tenure that push beyond the reductive dichotomy of renting versus owning; and how little political will there is to reform that system to allow more just forms of landownership to flourish in all markets.

CLTs continue to be criticized by skeptics for "not getting to scale," measured solely in terms of the number of housing units in a CLT's portfolio. A rejoinder to this narrow conception of scale has been offered by Zachary Murray of the Oakland CLT, who points out that many grassroots CLTs are seeking to elevate something far more fundamental: community control of land in places where, for generations, residents have been denied any sort of collective control over how land has been used or developed. It can also be said that scale should be measured *horizontally,* counting the number of communities that have adopted strategies that put land use decision-making and long-term control in the hands of residents who have been systematically and historically cut out of the frame.

To date, cold-market cities and neighborhoods have been an overlooked part of the horizontal potential and performance of CLTs. As the CLT model continues the long journey towards acceptance and professionalization, however, there exists an opportunity to apply the model in places and ways that go beyond its current hot-market focus on preserving the affordability of owner-occupied housing. In this context, cold markets are prime areas for CLT invention and exploration. They provide opportunities for community-led development on community-owned land that include more than housing;

opportunities to build resilient models of democratic participation and governance through which residents can influence current and *future* development; and opportunities to restore land justice in communities that have been harmed by government policy, market activity, and white supremacy. The road may be rockier in cold markets, but the long-term growth, vitality, and acceptance of the CLT movement demands a model that is inclusive and deployable in any market.

Notes

1. Susan Witt and Robert Swann, "Land: Challenge and Opportunity," Schumacher Center for a New Economics, May 1995. (*https://centerforneweconomics.org/publications/land-challenge-and-opportunity/*).

2. Alan Mallach, *The Divided City: Poverty and Prosperity in Urban America* (Washington, DC: Island Press, 2018).

3. Myungshik Choi, Shannon Van Zandt, and David Matarrita-Cascante, "Can community land trusts slow gentrification?" *Journal of Urban Affairs*, 40:3, 394-411 (2018).

4. Various terms are used throughout this essay to refer to cold-market areas, including struggling, declining, weak, divided, declining, or shrinking — mainly echoing the range of descriptors used in the voluminous literature on urban decline. Admittedly, these terms are imprecise and not necessarily synonyms. Note, too, that this essay does not take a position on geographic scale, recognizing that weak-market dynamics are relative and can play out at the neighborhood, city, and/or regional level.

5. John Emmeus Davis, "Homes That Last," *Shelterforce,* National Housing Institute, December 2008 (*https://shelterforce.org/2008/12/22/homes_that_last/*).

6. Emily Thaden, "Stable Home Ownership in a Turbulent Economy: Delinquencies and Foreclosures Remain Low in Community Land Trusts," Lincoln Institute of Land Policy, Working Paper WP11ET1, July 2011.

7. Max Blau, "Black Southerners Are Bearing the Brunt of America's Eviction Epidemic," Stateline [online], January 18, 2019 (*https://www.pewtrusts.org/en/research-and-analysis/blogs/stateline/2019/01/18/black-southerners-are-bearing-the-brunt-of-americas-eviction-epidemic*). T. Cookson, et. al., *Losing Home: The Human Cost of Eviction in Seattle,* A Report by the Seattle Women's Commission and the Housing Justice Project of the King County Bar Association, September 2018 (*https://www.kcba.org/Portals/0/pbs/pdf/Losing%20Home%202018.pdf*). Matthew Desmond, "Poor Black Women Are Evicted at Alarming Rates, Setting Off a Chain of Hardship," MacArthur Foundation Policy Research Brief, March 2014 (*https://www.macfound.org/media/files/HHM_Research_Brief_-_Poor_Black_Women_Are_Evicted_at_Alarming_Rates.pdf*).

8. The "displaced" are included here because there are many instances of people maintaining connections to neighborhoods from which they've been displaced. Folks who have been forced to move away from a neighborhood in which their families may have lived for several generations, frequently make the trek back to attend church, to shop, or to see family and friends. Many would welcome the chance to return — and a CLT might be a vehicle to facilitate their return. A handful of cities have adopted "right to return" policies or given housing preferences for displaced residents.

9. Existing groups can also be gatekeepers to accessing essential resources and knowledge or can be dismissive of innovative ideas and approaches — both common reactions to new CLT efforts in areas where the model is unfamiliar.

10. "Community-led development on community-owned land" aka "common ground" is John Davis' phrasing. John Emmeus Davis, "Common Ground: Community-Owned Land as a Platform for Equitable and Sustainable Development," *University of San Francisco Law Review,* Vol 51, No. 1, 2014.

11. Greg Rosenberg and Jeffrey Yuen have surveyed the field and compiled a useful compendium of both agricultural and commercial CLT projects. See Greg Rosenberg and Jeffrey Yuen, "Beyond Housing: Urban Agriculture and Commercial Development by Community Land Trusts," Lincoln Institute of Land Policy, Working Paper WP13GR1, 2012.

12. Athens Land Trust, "2017 Annual Report." (*https://athenslandtrust.org/wp-content/uploads/2019/01/2017-Annual-Report-1.2.19-1.pdf*).

13. For a discussion of opportunities and challenges for commercial CLT applications, see: Elizabeth Sorce, "The Role of Community Land Trusts in Preserving and Creating Commercial Assets: A Dual Case Study of Rondo CLT in St. Paul, Minnesota and Crescent City CLT in New Orleans, Louisiana" (2012). University of New Orleans Theses and Dissertations. Paper 1501 (*http://scholarworks.uno.edu/td/1501*).

14. See the Homebaked CLT website for more information: (*http://homebaked.org.uk/about/we_are_homebaked/*).

15. John Emmeus Davis, "Homes That Last," op. cit.

16. Services that are offered to residents who do not live in CLT housing may enable a CLT to diversify its revenues, gaining access to new sources funding.

17. Many CLTs adopt strong community organizing and political strategies in advance of — or alongside — actual real estate development work. For instance, TRUST South LA has a vibrant resident-centered transportation and mobility justice program that advocates for healthy, walkable, and "bikeable" streets — a major quality-of-life issue for residents of this Los Angeles neighborhood. In New Orleans, the Jane Place

Neighborhood Sustainability Initiative has advanced a robust advocacy agenda around the impacts of short-term rentals (such as AirBnB) on the growing affordability crisis, as a separate yet related component of their CLT work.

18. For a history of the early years of DSNI, see Peter Medoff and Holly Sklar, *Streets of Hope: The Fall and Rise of an Urban Neighborhood* (Boston, MA: South End Press, 1999) and *Holding Ground: The Rebirth of Dudley Street* [Video], directed by Mark Lipman and Leah Mahan, Holding Ground Productions, 1997.

19. Dudley Street Neighborhood Initiative, *From the Bottom Up: The Dudley Street Neighborhood Initiative Strategy for Sustainable Economic Development,* Unpublished Draft Manuscript, November 1997.

20. Eugene "Gus" Newport, *The Dudley Street Neighborhood Initiative, Roxbury, Massachusetts: History and Observations,* Unpublished Manuscript, July 1991.

21. On the concept of "just transition," see Movement Generation Justice and Ecology Project, *From Banks and Tanks to Cooperation and Caring: A Strategic Framework for a Just Transition.* (*https://movementgeneration.org/wp-content/uploads/2016/11/JT_booklet_Eng_printspreads.pdf*).

22. Kali Akuno, "Build and Fight: The Program and Strategy of Cooperation Jackson," in Cooperation Jackson (Kali Akuno, Sacajawea Hall, and Brandon King) and Ajamu Nangwaya (eds.), *Jackson Rising: The Struggle for Economic Democracy and Black Self-Determination in Jackson, Mississippi,* Daraja Press, 2017.

23. Hazel Sheffield, "Cooperation Jackson on How to Build an Alternative Economy for People of Colour," The Independent UK, May 31, 2019 (*https://www.independent.co.uk/news/business/indyventure/cooperation-jackson-solidarity-economy-neoliberalism-alternatives-a8936801.html*).

24. This has been correctly characterized as a new form of redlining — a systemic bias in both the government and finance sectors that are connected to real estate, housing, and social programs. See: John Emmeus Davis, "A New Kind of Redlining: Punishing Success," *Shelterforce,* May 6, 2013 (*https://shelterforce.org/2013/05/06/a_new_kind_of_redlining_punishing_success/*).

2.

Take a Stand, Own the Land

Dudley Neighbors Inc., a Community Land Trust in Boston, Massachusetts

Harry Smith and Tony Hernandez

Dudley Neighbors Inc. (DNI) is the community land trust formed in 1988 to serve the Roxbury-North Dorchester area of Boston, Massachusetts. DNI was an outgrowth of years of grassroots organizing and participatory planning by the Dudley Street Neighborhood Initiative (DSNI). These two organizations remain tightly intertwined, sharing staff, resources, and a corporate umbrella. More importantly, they share a mission and vision of comprehensive neighborhood revitalization in which community ownership of land and community empowerment of the area's residents go hand-in-hand.

This chapter details the conditions in the Dudley neighborhood that led to the creation of DSNI and the launch of the "Don't Dump on Us" campaign to address blighted vacant lots in the area. The success of those early anti-dumping campaigns led to a new campaign, "Take a Stand, Own the Land," and formation of the DNI community land trust. The chapter will describe how the community came together to create a comprehensive revitalization plan and to win eminent domain power from the City of Boston for vacant, blighted land in the Dudley Triangle. The authors will describe the strategies DSNI/DNI used to deeply engage residents in and around DNI's housing and will explain how the community-owned land in the DNI portfolio leverages the neighborhood's influence over public and private development throughout the neighborhood.

The chapter will conclude by detailing current efforts to acquire land outside of the original target area, partnering with the City of Boston and others to acquire private land and buildings to turn into mixed-use, affordable developments. DSNI is also playing a key role in supporting the formation of new CLTs in the Boston area and in helping to create a new city-wide organization to promote cooperation and coordination among all of Boston's CLTs, young and old: the Greater Boston CLT Network.

By sharing the lessons learned from thirty-five years of community organizing, planning, and development, the authors hope to contribute to the growth of the global CLT movement by highlighting the benefits of community control over land.

BACKGROUND

"Affordable housing in perpetuity through Dudley Neighbors Inc. is the gift that keeps on giving for families in our community. The land trust is a powerful tool guided by the voices of residents in low-income communities to ensure that housing is forever affordable and that land is used for the public good."—Sister Margaret Leonard, long-time DSNI board member

Located less than two miles from downtown Boston, the Dudley area of Roxbury-North Dorchester is a tri-lingual neighborhood of more than 25,000 African-American, Latin American, Cape Verdean, and White residents where English, Spanish and Cape Verdean Creole is spoken.

Dudley's population is among the poorest and youngest in Boston. Approximately 27% of the area's population falls below the poverty line, as defined by the federal government. More than 40% of the neighborhood's households earn less than $25,000 annually and the neighborhood's high unemployment rate of 15% is more than twice the city-wide average. A few other statistics set the stage for our story: 18% of Dudley's residents are 14–24 years of age; 40% of the neighborhood's households contain children who are younger than 18 years; 26% of adults in the neighborhood do not have a high school degree; and 62% of Dudley's households are considered "cost burdened" by virtue of spending more than 30% of their household's income for the housing they occupy.

THE BIRTH OF DSNI: "DON'T DUMP ON US!"

By the 1980s, Dudley contained a staggering amount of vacant land — a total of 1300 parcels — representing nearly a third of the acreage of the entire neighborhood. This was a consequence of three decades of disinvestment, redlining, abandonment, poorly planned urban renewal, and arson-for-profit. The neighborhood had also become an illegal dumping ground for trash from around the city and state. In the dead of night and in broad daylight, trucks would roll into the neighborhood and deposit on the neighborhood's vacant lots old cars, old refrigerators, rotten meat, toxic chemicals, and debris from construction sites.

"When I first came here, all I remember is trash and vacant lots and house fires," says Evelyn Correa, a current DSNI board member. "All of a sudden you would see a home go up in flames and we would say, 'That must have been for the insurance.'"

In 1984, the Riley Foundation, one of the larger charitable foundations in Massachusetts, decided to focus on the revitalization of Dudley after touring the neighborhood's most blighted sections with leaders of local nonprofit organizations. The Dudley Advisory Group was created, made up mostly of community development corporations and social services organizations doing work in the area. On October 15, 1984, with 22 people in attendance, the group voted unanimously to establish a new organization. Three months later, it was given the name of the "Dudley Street Neighborhood Initiative."

When the grand plans envisioned by this new initiative were first presented to the neighborhood, however, "all hell broke loose," as one of the participants in that roll-out meeting later described it. Neighborhood residents challenged the Advisory Group's assertion that this was to be an initiative of, by, and for the community. Local resident Che Madyun asked the Advisory Group, "How many of you people up there live in this neighborhood?" When only one hand was raised, there was an angry demand from the floor for resident control of the planning process — and of the organization itself.

This triggered a fundamental reconsideration of the assumptions behind DSNI, forcing the Dudley Advisory Group to go back to the drawing board. The Riley Foundation and the nonprofit organizations that had backed the original approach were quick to accept the demand for resident control. They immediately began weaving this principle into the bylaws being drafted for the new organization. A governing board with thirty-one members (later expanded to thirty-five) would have a resident majority. Minimum representation would be guaranteed for each of the neighborhood's four major cultures: African-American, Cape Verdean, Latino, and White.

The election of the inaugural board of directors occurred on April 27, 1985. More than 100 people were in attendance, filling the front pews of St. Patrick's Church. Local resident leaders were elected as the co-chairs. The following year, the board unanimously approved a new slate of officers, with Che Madyun being named DSNI's president.

In 1986, DSNI hired Peter Medoff, a veteran community organizer, as its first executive director. He won the job at DSNI because he emphasized the need for community organizing and community empowerment to remain at the center of the new organization's plans for the neighborhood's physical, social, and economic revitalization.

As the organization completed its initial process of extensive door knocking and surveying of local residents and merchants, it became clear that the issue of illegal dumping and blight was the issue where DSNI would need to start. The "Don't Dump on Us" campaign was created to clean up vacant lots, to stop illegal dumping, and to force government oversight of the large number of poorly regulated trash-transfer stations in the neighborhood. Residents organized their own clean-up efforts, while pushing the City of Boston to take greater responsibility for removing garbage, construction debris, and abandoned cars from City-owned and privately owned vacant lots.

TAKE A STAND, OWN THE LAND:
THE CREATION OF DUDLEY NEIGHBORS INC.

"DNI was created to carry out the neighborhood's redevelopment strategy. Instead of simply responding to plans created by private developers or the City, we created the community land trust as the vehicle to exercise community control over our land. The land trust helps us sustain our vision and make it a reality."—Bob Haas, long-time DSNI leader

By 1987, DSNI had successfully pressured the City to close three illegal trash-transfer stations and had made progress in cleaning up vacant lots. Leaders came to understand that in order to realize the dream of community revitalization, DSNI would need to move from organizing against harmful practices such as dumping to planning proactively for future development of the neighborhood. Only in this way would the community be able to break out of the deadly cycle of real estate speculation followed by disinvestment that had plagued the area for decades. After an intensive process of bottom-up participatory planning, DSNI completed The Dudley Street Neighborhood Comprehensive Revitalization Plan, which laid out a blueprint for rebuilding the neighborhood. At its center was an overall commitment to development without displacement. DSNI then wielded the community power it had built over the course of earlier organizing campaigns to convince the City of Boston to abandon the master plan that had been drafted by city officials and to adopt DSNI's community-generated plan as its own.

Two years later, DSNI made history by becoming the first and only community-based organization in the United States to win the power of eminent domain. DSNI had begun assembling the funds to implement its Comprehensive Revitalization Plan, including the promise of a $2 million Program Related Investment from the Ford Foundation. But absentee owners of the neighborhood's vacant parcels were reluctant to sell their land to DSNI. They had caught the scent of potential profits in the air. The City of Boston was in the process of rebuilding the subway line on the neighborhood's western edge, a massive investment in public infrastructure. Private speculators had taken note and begun to buy up lands and buildings in the neighborhood.

In 1988 when the DNI community land trust was formed, approximately thirty of the sixty-four acres of land in the Dudley Triangle consisted of blighted, vacant lots, with fifteen acres owned by the City of Boston and fifteen acres owned by private individuals or corporations. Because of the organizing and advocacy of DSNI, city officials were willing to transfer the fifteen acres of City-owned land to DNI. However, because the City-owned land was scattered among the privately-owned lots, DSNI's leaders realized that it would be a nearly impossible task to assemble enough contiguous land to carry out the community's development vision. The majority of the private holdings were tax delinquent, but given the length of the tax foreclosure process, it would take years to acquire these parcels. In order to more quickly achieve a critical mass of land for development, the organization decided that acquiring the privately-owned land by eminent domain was the only way to accomplish their ambitious urban village plan.

DSNI's leaders began a new campaign of grassroots organizing in 1989, as they lobbied Mayor Flynn and the Boston Redevelopment Authority (BRA) to grant DSNI the power to assemble contiguous sites that were large enough for building the affordable housing contemplated in the Comprehensive Revitalization Plan. "Take a Stand, Own the Land" was the campaign button that was distributed throughout the neighborhood. Residents were asking for the legal right to compel the absentee owners of vacant land in the central part of the neighborhood, the 64-acre Dudley Triangle, to sell their land for a fair price to DSNI. On November 10, 1989, the BRA board voted unanimously to grant the power of eminent domain to DSNI.

On the advice of DSNI's attorney, David Abromowitz, who was made available on a *pro bono* basis by one of Boston's most prestigious law firms, DSNI established a subsidiary corporation in 1988, Dudley Neighbors Inc. Structured and operated as a community land trust, DNI was set up not only to exercise the power of eminent domain in acquiring land within the Dudley Triangle; it was also established to retain ownership of land forever, holding it in trust for present and future generations.

> How do you avoid displacing the very people you are trying to help?

By holding onto the land — and by employing long-lasting ground leases to control the use and resale of whatever was built on its land — DNI positioned itself to be the permanent steward of affordable housing, commercial space, and other buildings that, in time, were to be constructed on its parcels. The goal, in every case, was to maintain the affordability of these buildings forever, while also preventing foreclosures during downturns in the local economy.

Community-owned land was to be an antidote to the ultimate dilemma of community development: How do you avoid displacing the very people you are trying to help? In the words of Paul Yelder, the first director of Dudley Neighbors Inc., "How do you improve a neighborhood, but still make it accessible, make it affordable?"

Placing the community land trust within a subsidiary corporation allowed DSNI to maintain its focus on community organizing and participatory planning, while ensuring that the community's vision and plans were carried out. In 1990, as a new decade began, DSNI adopted a new slogan, "Building Houses and People Too," highlighting its commitment to a holistic approach to Dudley's revitalization. The construction of affordable housing, parks, and playgrounds was a priority; but community organizing was deemed to be just as important.

BUILDING AN URBAN VILLAGE IN
THE DUDLEY TRIANGLE AND BEYOND

"I'm a city girl. I appreciate having a house in Boston that I can afford. And especially with the prices of houses now, I don't know how people could afford it. The fact that I got my house is a blessing."—Diane Dujon, DNI homeowner

Through the use of eminent domain and a deep partnership with the City of Boston, DNI had managed to acquire nearly all of the public and private vacant lots in the Dudley Triangle by 2019, giving the land trust control of more than thirty of the sixty-four acres in the Triangle. These vacant lots have been transformed into 227 high-quality, permanently affordable homes — including owner-occupied houses, cooperatives, and nonprofit rentals. The land trust's holdings also include two acres of community farms, a greenhouse, and neighborhood parks, playgrounds, gardens, commercial space, and other amenities of the urban village that Dudley residents had envisioned as they were organizing to clean up vacant lots.

The creation of hundreds of new, permanently affordable homes over the last 25 years on the sites of formerly abandoned, blighted lots has had an incredible impact on the Dudley community. The homes include ninety-seven homeownership units, seventy-seven limited-equity cooperative units, and fifty-three rental units, reflecting the desire to provide housing opportunities to families with a broad range of incomes. In accordance with the neighborhood plan, the majority of rental, cooperative, and ownership units have three bedrooms and are targeted to families earning between 30%–60% of Area Median Income, approximately $30,000–$60,000 for a family of four. In fact, recent surveys of families living in DNI homeownership units show that more than half of the families earn less than $40,000/year, and yet are able to enjoy the benefits of owning their own homes.

The resale formula employed by DNI on homeownership units places an emphasis on stability and long-term ownership, with an owner's equity increasing each year that the owner stays in the home.

The positive impact of the revitalization of the Dudley Triangle can be measured in many ways: improved public safety; higher rates of homeownership, compared with the surrounding community; and a high level of resident satisfaction, as reported in the regular quality-of-life surveys that DSNI conducts.

"My dream was always to own my own home, but with the housing situation in Boston, everything was always so expensive," says Evelyn Correa, who was able to buy a home on the land trust in 2010 and has served as president of the Dudley Neighbors Inc. board for the past five years. "Now I just love having my little house. I hope to hand it down to my kids."

Fig. 2.1. Neighborhood revitalization, Dennis Street to Winthrop Street, before and after.

Diane Dujon, another homeowner in the land trust who has lived in Roxbury and Dorchester her whole life, says that one of the most important things to her about the land trust is that "it stabilizes the neighborhood. Once people move into their home, they don't leave, so I know my neighbors. We watch out for each other and help each other out."

Stabilization is a consequence of stewardship. DNI is able to preserve the affordability of any homes that are built on its land, no matter how hot Boston's real estate market may become. But there is also stability that comes from DNI's ongoing support for its homeowners and renters, helping them to stay in their homes, even when the economy goes bad. DNI staff build trusting relationships with residents and lenders. When necessary, DNI will invoke its power of "Consent to Mortgage" to prevent predatory lenders from marketing a destabilizing mortgage product in the Dudley neighborhood. The impact of this level of engagement and oversight is dramatic: while the larger neighborhood suffered more than two hundred foreclosures during the Great Recession, 2008–2013, there were no foreclosures of DNI homes over the same span of time. The entire portfolio has had only four foreclosures in 25 years, making the land trust an island of stability in a volatile real estate market. This is consistent with the performance of CLT homes across the nation. From 2008–2010, during the height of the foreclosure crisis, fewer than 1% of CLT homes across the country were foreclosed on, compared to 5% of total mortgage loans.

In keeping with the community's vision of an urban village, DNI has also stepped up efforts to develop retail and commercial spaces on land that it owns. DNI is currently partnering with a local community development corporation to build a commercial building on one of the last vacant lots in the Triangle. This project will fill a large gap in the business district and provide opportunities for new retail spaces to meet the needs of local residents.

As the final vacant lots in the Dudley Triangle have been developed and as the red-hot Boston real estate market has brought new threats to the stability of the Dudley neighborhood, DNI leaders have developed new strategies to add housing and commercial spaces to the land trust's portfolio. The most dramatic step was taken in 2017 when DNI acquired a former bank building in nearby Upham's Corner, with acquisition funds and technical support provided by the City of Boston. It was an historic move for the land trust, as it marked the first significant purchase of a property by DNI in many years and the first major acquisition of property outside of the Dudley Triangle. The goal of the project is to develop a mixed-use building that will include affordable housing, some of which will be reserved for artists, commercial space, and cultural spaces. This project will further the community's vision to transform Upham's Corner into an "Arts Innovation District" that will include the revitalization of the Strand Theater and the creation of a new public library. Because of DNI's successful track record, residents are hopeful that it will be possible to improve neighborhood arts amenities without raising rents and without displacing local families, businesses, and artists who have built the culture of Upham's Corner for generations.

In addition to pursuing new housing and commercial development opportunities, DNI is also utilizing the land trust model to promote community development through urban agriculture. Urban farms and gardens have always been a part of the vision and plan for revitalizing the Dudley neighborhood, a strategy to increase access to local food and to create open spaces that benefit the community. In 2004, DNI built a 10,000 square-foot community greenhouse on the site of a former auto body shop. DNI owns the underlying land and leases out the greenhouse to a local nonprofit partner, The Food Project, along with nearly two acres of urban farmland. The Food Project trains young people to operate farms and to organize farmers' markets serving neighborhood residents. DNI has also partnered with the Urban Farming Institute (UFI) to develop new neighborhood farms that will be managed by local residents who have graduated from UFI's farmer training program. The land trust model provides long-term stability to groups leading the urban farming movement in Boston and helps to fulfill the community's desire for open space and access to healthier food.

Fig. 2.2. Greenhouses operated by The Food Project on land leased from Dudley Neighbors Inc.

PUTTING THE "C" IN COMMUNITY LAND TRUST

"Many scholars and housing activists view market forces and housing affordability as mutually antagonistic: either a community remains affordable for its low-income residents, or it attracts capital investment, development and growth. If there is a way out of this fundamental contradiction, Boston's Dudley Street Neighborhood Initiative (DSNI) has found it. . . . The strong organizing base of the DSNI has created a unique resident-driven model of planning. This is in stark contrast to the conventional path by which city government develops a master plan before seeking community input."

—Fannie Mae Foundation, "Just-Right Neighborhoods" (2000)

From the founding of the organization, DSNI leaders realized that cleaning up lots and stopping illegal dumping were not enough. Without community control over planning and land use decisions, the neighborhood's residents would just continue to react to the next threat that came down the road. During that time, the City of Boston had in fact developed a master plan for the Dudley neighborhood, but they had neglected to involve community residents in their planning process. DSNI's "Take a Stand, Own the Land" campaign and the planning that accompanied it resulted in the City tearing up its plan and endorsing the DSNI vision. For the first time in Boston, residents, merchants, and youth — most of whom had never been engaged in urban planning — were able to come together to develop a plan that incorporated the principle of "development without displacement" into a City-approved master plan.

> Intensive focus on community engagement and leadership development is the key to DSNI's long-term success.

Thirty-five years later, DSNI and its community land trust are still organizing and involving both the people who live in DNI's housing and the people who live in the surrounding neighborhood. This intensive focus on community engagement and leadership development is the key to DSNI's long-term success and highlights one of the biggest impacts of successful CLTs. Rather than focusing only on the success and maintenance of CLT properties, DSNI integrates CLT residents into its organizing and planning initiatives to build community power and to improve the quality of life for the whole neighborhood.

DSNI's leaders view the CLT model as one of a number of tools they use to ensure strong resident engagement in land use decisions over the long-term. Through its Sustainable Development Committee, which reviews all private development projects to assess their adherence to the neighborhood's development vision, DSNI has been able to organize residents to shape private development in the neighborhood, ensuring that projects meet the standards established in DSNI's community plans, including affordable housing and access to local jobs.

"In addition to getting involved in CLT activities, land trust residents also serve on the board and committees of DSNI and play leadership roles on issues across the neighborhood," according to Tony Hernandez, Director of Dudley Neighbors Inc. "In this way, the CLT is able to be an effective steward of the land, while remaining in service to DSNI's larger vision of development without displacement and community control of the land."

Although winning eminent domain authority by the City has been rightly viewed as one of the major accomplishments of DSNI, there have been other lesser-known mechanisms that have sustained DSNI's power over private development in Dudley. For example, in 1999, DSNI and the City's Department of Neighborhood Development signed a Memorandum of Understanding that stipulated that DSNI would conduct the community planning process for City-owned land in the Dudley neighborhood. In the Dudley neighborhood, DSNI and the City continue to jointly convene community land use and housing design meetings, issue requests for proposals, and designate developers.

The combination of DSNI's role as community planner and DNI's stewardship of land means that residents are fully engaged in land use decisions in a large portion of the neighborhood. In the words of a long-time DSNI board member, "Developing a shared vision is absolutely crucial. By developing a shared vision, people come to sense that anything is possible. People really come to believe that." The results of this deep engagement are clear: in addition to the 227 homes that have been built on DNI's land, nearly 1,000 affordable homes have been produced or preserved elsewhere in the neighborhood by other nonprofit and for-profit developers because of DSNI's organizing and advocacy, an effort led by the organization's Sustainable Development Committee. This is a reflection of DSNI's power to affect land uses throughout the neighborhood.

SUPPORTING THE CITY-WIDE GROWTH
AND SUSTAINABILITY OF CLTs

Despite the successes of the community in creating and preserving affordable housing through the land trust and larger advocacy efforts, the Dudley neighborhood is dealing with new threats as the development boom in Boston intensifies. Resident-led improvements have led to the neighborhood facing outside investors seeking opportunities for development and new, wealthier residents moving in. The opportunity for DNI to acquire vacant parcels of land at little or no cost is a thing of the past, as private developers move into sections of the neighborhood they would not have touched a decade ago. These circumstances are not unique to Dudley; similar patterns are apparent across Boston and neighboring towns. In response, DSNI and ten neighborhood groups from across the city launched the Greater Boston Community Land Trust Network in 2015. The goal of this regional effort is to expand the CLT model and to work with allies to make a city-wide push for the kind of community control over land disposition, ownership, and development that has been won in the Dudley neighborhood.

"This launch is coming at a critical moment in Boston history," said Harry Smith, DSNI's former Director of Sustainable Economic Development, speaking at the press conference announcing the Network's creation. "As one of the fastest-gentrifying cities in the United States, we're here to either claim the future of our neighborhoods . . . or risk losing them to gentrification and displacement."

With the formation of the Greater Boston Community Land Trust Network, DSNI is working towards its goal of building the capacity of partners in other neighborhoods to develop resident-led plans, to control land-use decisions, and to take ownership of land in their own communities. Over the past year, several new CLTs have formed in the Boston area with the Network's support and assistance, including the Chinatown CLT, Somerville CLT, Boston Neighborhood CLT, and the Urban Farming CLT, creating a sense of momentum and solidarity across multiple neighborhoods. With a growing membership, the Network is also serving as a vehicle to advocate for municipal policies and public resources that will promote development without displacement across the entire city.

CONCLUSION

In the documentary film, *Arc of Justice,* Charles Sherrod, one of the founders of New Communities Inc., the nation's first CLT, says, "All power comes from the land." This is undoubtedly true. At the same time, the experience of DSNI and the DNI bears witness to the political reality that the reverse is true as well: "All land comes from community power." The leaders of DSNI and DNI have come to believe that the only way to realize the community's vision over the long-term is to meld the community ownership and governance features of the CLT with sustained organizing and planning in order to get land and to use it wisely for the benefit of the entire community.

As DNI's Director, Tony Hernandez says, "Without a clear vision and development plan that has been created by neighborhood residents and without structures in place to monitor and to oversee the development of that vision, the CLT will not be effective in the long run." Or, in the words of a long-time community leader, "Usually we, the community, are fighting to have a seat at the table to fight for affordability and avoid displacement. But because of the land trust, I'm proud to say that we not only have a seat at the table, we *own* the table."

3.

Origins and Evolution of Urban Community Land Trusts in Canada

Susannah Bunce and Joshua Barndt

The development of community land trusts in Canada offers an interesting study of the often individualized and ad hoc processes involved in CLT creation. While certainly not as numerous as CLTs in the USA and England, CLTs in Canada have burgeoned over the past several decades. They have been on the forefront of addressing affordable housing shortages and offered new ways to consider community land stewardship in Canada. The earliest CLTs were primarily located in Canadian cities, established as independent land trust initiatives through cooperative housing organizations, and as responses to affordable housing challenges in cities such as Montreal, Toronto, Winnipeg, and Vancouver. More recently, there has been an increasingly robust and more formalized network of CLTs emerging across Canada in response to on-going affordable housing shortages, gentrification processes, and a renewed interest in community-led practices that extend beyond affordable housing provision. Our chapter explores the historical appearance of CLTs in Canadian cities and why they continue to be an important community-led, non-governmental organizational model in a nation where government has traditionally played the leading role in the provision of affordable housing and social services.

Despite Canada's social democratic roots, different levels of government have been actively dismantling social programs over the last several decades, including a withdrawal from the funding and delivery of social housing programs starting in the early 1990s (Hulchanski 2001, 2007; Leone and Carole, 2010; Moore and Skaburskis, 2004; Wolfe, 1998).[1] Increasing governmental reliance on the private, for-profit sector for the delivery of housing and fiscal cutbacks to social services have had a detrimental impact on both housing affordability and the presence of social and community-based programs.[2]

Community-led CLT organizations have emerged within the context of these broader political-economic transformations in Canada, which have shaped the organizational structure, community actions, and programming of CLTs over time.

We identify two "generations" of community land trust organizations in Canada — the first being a small group of CLTs, arising in the 1980s to around 2012, that were largely focused on the acquisition of land for affordable housing provision. These CLT organizations, inspired by the CLT model in the United States, differed from land trust organizing in Canada that had traditionally focused on the conservation of wilderness and agricultural areas. The emergence of this new form of land trust in Canadian cities occurred within the context of a lack of public policy and legislative support for the creation of CLTs. As a result, they were primarily formed by cooperative housing federations, non-profit developers, and activist groups, often in partnership with specific governmental affordable housing programs.

A "second generation" of CLTs has emerged since 2012, both as a response to increasing gentrification pressures in urban areas and as a result of renewed interest in affordable housing development. New CLTs have emerged in cities such as Toronto and Vancouver,

> Canadian CLT development has been eclectic, sometimes incorporating features of the American model and sometimes not.

for example, cities that have experienced a steady rise in single-family homeownership and property speculation over the past decade, along with quickly rising housing prices and increased constraints on already tight affordable rental housing markets (Gee, 2017; King, 2016; McClearn, 2017). These second-generation CLTs have forged connections with existing and new CLT organizations across Canada and have interacted with an emergent international CLT movement. Locally, the activism of these CLT organizations has often extended beyond the land trust model itself, responding to broader urban issues such as the impact of rapid gentrification and displacement, decreases in affordable housing supply, advocacy for urban food security, and solidarity with racialized and culturally diverse communities, including building allyship with Indigenous peoples. These second-generation CLT organizations are distinguished by new approaches to the development and provision of communal and shared equity housing, by varied forms of neighbourhood and city-wide activism, and by a community land trust network being built across Canada.

Our chapter traces the evolution of Canadian CLTs and underlines the importance of their self-identification as CLTs in structuring their own organizations and operations. More often than not, Canadian CLT organizations view themselves as being a community land trust regardless of whether they exhibit all the characteristics of the traditional or "classic" CLT, as that model has been defined and implemented in the United States. The American "classic" model was premised on: a two-party ownership structure, whereby the CLT acts as the owner and long-term lessor for multiple parcels of land underneath buildings that are separately owned by individuals, cooperatives, or other nonprofit or for-profit entities; an organizational structure with a tripartite board and a place-based membership that emphasizes the participation of CLT residents, local community members, and members of the public; and an operational commitment to the permanent affordability of any housing located on the CLT's land, along with other stewardship duties designed to protect the condition of the structures and the security of tenure for the occupants (Davis, 2007; 2010). By comparison, Canadian CLT development has been more ad hoc and eclectic, sometimes incorporating these "classic" features and sometimes not, depending on their individual contexts and familiarity with the American CLT model. As such, Canadian CLTs have forged "home-grown" CLT characteristics that are primarily constituted by the very localized circumstances of their formation.

We trace the evolution of CLT development in Canada in a chronological way, through a narrative of the organizational objectives and projects of first- and second-generation CLTs. The CLTs that are discussed are organizations with which we are familiar, as CLT researchers and practitioners, and which offer certain insights into the origins and evolution of CLTs in the Canadian context. We conclude by suggesting that a steady increase in the presence of CLTs in Canada has necessitated the creation of formalized networks of knowledge transfer and information sharing in order to build solidarity and connections among CLT organizations and communities across Canada. An example of this is the recent emergence of the Canadian CLT Network that is fostering regular communication among CLT organizations across the country.

THE FIRST GENERATION OF CANADIAN CLTs
1980s–2012

A defining characteristic of this first cluster of largely sector-based CLTs,[3] which emerged from the 1980s to 2012, was the primary focus on the provision of cooperative and other forms of affordable housing through land ownership by the CLT organization. The emphasis on co-op housing provision derived from the strong Canadian cooperative housing movement that started in the 1930s (Hulchanski, 1988) and became a dominant affordable housing model in cities in the 1970s, with the development of well-regarded co-op housing projects such as St. Lawrence in Toronto and with the support of housing activists and municipal, provincial, and federal governments for this form of housing.

The CLT model, adopted through informal activist knowledge of the American CLT movement, became a conduit through which affordable housing, primarily co-op housing, was produced at a localized scale. We also observe a notable difference in the size and scope of CLTs during this period. Some CLTs, such as Colandco in Toronto and the Vernon District Community Land Trust in Vernon, British Columbia, adopted a sector-based and city-wide organizational approach with little community-led direction over the CLT organization itself. Conversely, other CLTs such as the West Broadway CLT embraced a more community-led, neighbourhood-based approach in the provision of affordable housing.

Colandco (Toronto)

The first two CLTs in Canada, both formed in the 1980s, focused on the provision of cooperative housing: Colandco in Toronto and Milton-Parc in Montreal. Colandco (initially called Inner City) was established in 1986 as a land holding and sector-based development company by the Co-operative Housing Federation of Toronto. Colandco purchased existing rental apartment buildings as well as parcels of land for the purpose of developing new multi-unit residential projects. Colandco retained ownership of the land and the buildings, while executing a 49-year lease with each cooperative for both. This arrangement provided the co-ops with use of the properties for the term of the lease. By retaining long-term ownership and control of the land and buildings, Colandco could ensure that the housing would remain affordable in perpetuity (Communitas Inc. 1985; Hulchanski, 1983; Interview with Tom Clement, February 18, 2019).

Colandco successfully leveraged its initial $2 million (CAD) of seed funding to develop an initial project,[4] the City Park Co-op, that secured 770 cooperative housing units through the acquisition of a privately owned rental project that was in receivership. Using the revolving fund as a deposit to secure the site, Colandco was subsequently able to mobilize funding and financing from the provincial government to complete the $63 million purchase. By the early 1990s, Colandco had assembled land ownership on a large scale for the development of fourteen housing cooperatives, containing a total of 2,350 housing units scattered across central Toronto, Scarborough, and Oshawa (Canada Mortgage and Housing Corporation, 2005; Co-operative Housing Federation of Toronto, 2019).

Colandco's program of land expansion and residential development started to face challenges in 1994, however, as a result of a global financial recession that began in the early 1990s and was significantly felt for several years in the province of Ontario. The withdrawal of governmental support for social housing and other affordable housing programs during the same period also impacted Colandco's projects. These pressures caused Colandco to downsize its housing development activities and to focus increasingly on retaining land ownership through a land trust arrangement with individual co-operatives (Canada Mortgage and Housing Corporation, 2005; Hulchanski 1983). Colandco entered into contractual agreements with individual nonprofit housing cooperatives to operate housing on its land, an approach that has had significant success and longevity in Toronto.

In 2017, Colandco and the Co-operative Housing Federation of Toronto took the lead in forming the Co-op Housing Land Trusts, consisting of four different land trusts: Colandco; the Bathurst Quay Co-op; Colandco's City Park Co-op; the Naismith Non-Profit Land Trust; and the Tenants Non-Profit Redevelopment Foundation (TNRC). These land trusts operate as a group. With the exception of the Bathurst Quay Co-op, each land trust has the same Board of Directors. Importantly, each land trust owns the land that is occupied by its cooperatives. As the leasee, each co-op is responsible for the management of its buildings. At the end of the land lease, the buildings will be transferred to the land trust unless the lease is renewed.

As a whole, the cooperatives that constitute the Co-op Housing Land Trusts are made up of thirty-two buildings, containing a total of 4,196 apartments or houses that are occupied by approximately 10,000 residents (Correspondence with Tom Clement, 2019). It is important to note that co-op residents are not organizational members of the Co-op Housing Land Trusts, but remain members of their individual cooperatives. This arrangement points to an innovative utilization of the community land trust model, where particular aspects of the CLT, such as land ownership and ground lease agreements, are combined with the autonomy of the co-op buildings. Resident members govern their individual cooperatives, but they may or may not have any involvement with the entity that owns the underlying land.

Communaute Milton-Parc (Montreal)

The Milton-Parc community, located in the downtown core of Montreal, has had similar success and longevity in the production of cooperative housing, while putting a creative, homegrown spin on the traditional CLT model. The idea for Communaute Milton-Parc (CMP) emerged from a lengthy resident-led and community-based struggle to save the neighbourhood from urban renewal plans proposed by a consortium of Montreal-based property developers. The activism of the Milton Parc Citizens Committee in the late 1960s and 1970s, which included street sit-ins and the occupation of buildings slated for demolition, succeeded in halting the renewal plans. The activists then formed multiple cooperative housing communities to purchase and to renovate the buildings, preserving this housing for low-income and middle-income residents (Kowaluk and Piche-Burton, 2012; Roussopoulos and Hawley, 2018).[5]

A growing concern about gentrification and displacement in the 1980s then led to the creation of the Communaute Milton-Parc in 1986. Approved by Quebec's provincial government, the CMP was viewed by the individual cooperatives as a way to protect housing affordability by protecting and stewarding the neighbourhood's land. Land titles in Milton-Parc are collectively owned by a syndicate of fifteen individual cooperatives and six nonprofit housing corporations through a Declaration of Co-Ownership. The CMP is governed by a general assembly constituted by the syndicate of co-owners. CMP acts as a governing and community decision-making body that regulates and sets guiding policy for cooperative ownership and community responsibility. CMP also owns and maintains the land beneath the common areas and enforces non-speculative restrictions on land uses and any land sales that might be contemplated by an individual cooperative (Ibid.).

Fig. 3.1. The Milton Parc neighbourhood, Montreal. OLIVIA WILLIAMS

CMP is an innovative take on the traditional structure of the CLT model. In the latter, the use of land and the affordability of housing are regulated through a ground lease for land that is owned by the CLT. Communaute Milton-Parc, by contrast, does not own the land beneath the housing itself but works as an overarching governance body for the Milton Parc neighbourhood that presently includes 148 buildings, 616 affordable units, and 1500 residents (Milton Parc, 2013). As a governance and decision-making body, the CMP arrangement offers a uniquely localized arrangement in which land is utilized and regulated in a way that best suits the preferences and circumstances of a particular neighbourhood. The organization has, over time, put in place a fulsome governance structure with a sophisticated assemblage of decision-making protocols and community engagement practices that connect the individual cooperatives and the overarching CMP body. This is combined with a focus on stopping residential displacement and supporting the longevity of affordable cooperative housing.

Milton Parc is the single largest cooperative housing neighbourhood in North America. Its size and success made Communaute Milton-Parc a finalist in the UN World Habitat Awards in 2013 (CMHC, 2005; World Habitat, 2017). Today, Milton Parc's residents remain active in public discussions about gentrification, displacement, and the need for affordable housing in Montreal. Importantly, they self-identify and publicly characterize their unique combination of fifteen cooperative housing communities, a single landholding syndicate, and an overarching structure of governance as being a community land trust.

CLT Formation in Central and Western Canada

In Colandco, the Co-op Housing Land Trusts, and Communaute Milton-Parc, we observe an emphasis on and support for long-term retention of affordable housing, whereby land trust arrangements serve as an innovative platform for producing and preserving housing that is cooperatively owned and managed. There was a similar focus on affordable housing provision among the community land trust organizations that arose in central and western Canada from the mid-1990s to mid-2000s. Without the existence of a formalized CLT network and, in most cases, without the existence of government legislation that would have legitimized or supported the existence of CLTs, such development tended to be ad hoc and localized.[6]

These CLTs were initiated by community activists who were searching for alternative, practical methods by which to attain affordable housing. They focused on individual homeownership, rather than cooperative housing, while working in partnership with private, for-profit developers and philanthropic affordable housing developers such as Habitat for Humanity. There is also evidence of informal knowledge sharing among these Canadian CLT organizers, who sometimes drew on personal information gathered about the implementation of the CLT model in the United States (Bunce, Khimani, *et al*, 2013).

West Broadway Community Land Trust (WBCLT) was the earliest example. It was established in 1999 as a subsidiary of the West Broadway Community Development Corporation (CMHC, 2005), located in the West Broadway neighbourhood of downtown Winnipeg, Manitoba. The community development corporation was a particularly innovative community development organization that focused on affordable housing and other social initiatives such as a community credit union, and was guided by concerns over local poverty issues caused by public disinvestment and encroaching gentrification/rising residential prices (Beaubien and Ring, 2006).

The intention of the WBCLT was to provide more diverse affordable housing tenure options in the form of rent-to-own homeownership, individual homeownership, cooperative homeownership, and affordable rental units (CMHC, 2005). A 2006 study of the WBCLT noted, however, that the primary focus of WBCLT was rent-to-own homeownership, addressing the needs of low-income households who were unable to move directly into homeownership but who might become homeowners over time with assistance (Beaubien and Ring, 2006). WBCLT assembled neighbourhood land parcels and purchased existing housing stock over a five-year period, offering a rent-to-own plan that was secured through a ground lease agreement between WBCLT and the tenant (who was also the potential owner).

This arrangement entailed the oversight of extensive renovations and the management of a complex array of funding from different governmental housing programs (Ibid., p. 3). Ultimately, WBCLT was unable to sustain the organizational and funding capacity that was needed both to undertake these renovations and to maintain the units through the duration of the rent-to-own period. This resulted in the eventual closure of the WBCLT as an arm of the West Broadway Community Development Corporation and the sale of some of its housing at market rate. Despite this failure, as Beaubien and Ring (Ibid.) noted, WBCLT played an important role in galvanizing community engagement and increasing public debate about land tenure as a component of community development, having a positive and lasting significance for the West Broadway community.

Other first-generation CLTs in central and western Canada faced similar challenges. The *Vernon and District Community Land Trust Society* (VDCLT) was formed in the province of British Columbia in 2008 to accrue public and philanthropic donations of lands and buildings for the development and management of affordable housing (Vernon and District Community Land Trust Society, 2012). The VDCLT's first project was a joint initiative with the City of Vernon, whereby the local government purchased land near the downtown core that was leased to the VDCLT through a long-term contractual arrangement and a small lease payment. The VDCLT, with Habitat for Humanity as a development partner, subsequently constructed rental units for low-income families and people with disabilities on this site. Since this initial project, the VDCLT has focused its efforts on accruing title to other lands and attaining public and philanthropic funding for additional affordable housing projects. It remains engaged with local communities in advocating for affordable housing in Vernon.

Also appearing in western Canada during this period was the *Calgary Community Land Trust* (CCLT). The CCLT was formed by the Calgary Homeless Foundation and was incorporated as a nonprofit organization in 2003 (Canada Mortgage and Housing Corporation, 2005). The CCLT focused on the assembly of land and building stock, as well as obtaining funds for the development and operation of affordable housing (Calgary Community Land Trust, 2012). CCLT received a donation of surplus federal government land, the result of a land swap between the federal government and the municipal government of Calgary, acquired for the purpose of building affordable housing on the land. The CCLT's first affordable housing project was the Sun Court development, completed in 2007, consisting of 27 units of owner-occupied family housing built by Habitat for Humanity Calgary (Calgary Homeless Foundation, 2012). The CCLT then went dormant for several years, as the work of the Calgary Homeless Foundation shifted towards more immediate and front-line initiatives to address homelessness in Calgary. It is now functioning as a CLT again, as we will discuss in the next section, reporting on more recent Canadian CLTs.

The *Central Edmonton Community Land Trust* (CECLT) emerged as a nonprofit corporation in 1998 with a mandate of fostering community-based development through land management and affordable housing provision. CECLT received donated land and properties from the municipal government of Edmonton and received funding from philanthropic foundations and development loans from the federal government's Canada Mortgage and Housing Corporation and Edmonton's Inner-City Housing Society. Unfortunately, due to difficulties in securing mortgages in the rent-to-own arrangements, CECLT had to repay Edmonton's government for the cost of the donated properties, selling them at market rate in order to raise reimbursement funds.

The situation in Edmonton highlights some of the broader challenges that were faced by the early CLTs in Canada, including: an inability to obtain mortgages for CLT home-owners; reliance on piecemeal and unpredictable government funding; and shifting political support for CLT activities from local government.

There were major differences among the CLTs that formed during this period, both in the tenure and scale of their projects and in the extent to which organizations and their activities were led by a place-based community. Some of these efforts, such as Milton-Parc and the West Broadway CLT, were community-led at the neighbourhood level, while the majority of CLTs during this period were driven by sector-based organizations such as the Co-operative Housing Federation of Canada (in the case of Colandco) and the Calgary Homeless Foundation (in the case of the Calgary Community Land Trust). Despite the small number of CLTs that emerged prior to 2012, however, they contributed to an emerging public awareness about the model's potential for delivering affordable housing (see Canada Mortgage and Housing Corporation, 2005). They also shaped a path for the formation of a second wave of CLT organizations.

THE SECOND GENERATION OF CANADIAN CLTs
2012–PRESENT

There has been a resurgence of interest in CLT development in Canada in recent years. Out of twenty currently active CLTs in Canada, nine were established since 2014. In 2017, moreover, a new Canadian CLT Network was formed to organize a more cohesive sector. This resurgence has been driven in part by the dynamic evolution of the small group of "first-generation," sector-based land trusts, which have re-emerged as expert-led nonprofit affordable housing developers. It also includes a new and energized "second generation" of more activist-based, community-based CLTs. The activists behind these latter initiatives — neighbourhood residents, community agencies, radical planners and, in some cases, municipal staff — have organized CLTs in response to the escalating affordable housing crisis in Canadian cities, rapid gentrification, and a renewed interest in community-based responses to these problems. While contemporary Canadian CLTs from both phases of CLT development share a common objective of increasing the supply of permanently affordable housing, they differ in their respective approaches to community-led development, community ownership, and democratic governance. We explore these issues in the following sections by referring to the activities of several representative second-generation CLTs.

Community-Based CLT Development

Since 2014, nine new community-led CLTs have emerged in response to an escalating affordable housing crisis in Canadian cities and a growing sense that government and social sector responses have been inadequate. This crisis, driven by an undersupply of housing, the increasing financialization of the housing market, and the repositioning by corporate landlords and private developers of existing housing for higher-income renters and homeowners, has translated into gentrification and redevelopment pressures in particular urban neighbourhoods (August and Walks, 2018; Bunce, 2018; Walks, 2014). For low-income and vulnerable residents, gentrification is a harmful process of destabilization. It causes food insecurity, housing insecurity, eviction, and displacement. While the social costs of gentrification are well known, neither the government nor the social housing sector has cultivated an adequate response. As a result, some impacted communities have looked to the community land trust as a way to mitigate gentrification.

The CLT model is appealing because of its emphasis on removing land and housing from the speculative market and controlling the rapid rise in real estate costs, thereby securing the perpetual affordability of land and housing. As Dominique Russell of the Kensington Market Land Trust in downtown Toronto's historic and gentrifying Kensington Market neighbourhood has stated, "Gentrification is a real estate problem and we felt we needed a real estate solution" (Interview with Dominique Russell, February 2, 2019, Toronto). Similar to first-generation CLTs, the current generation of community-led CLTs is focused on securing community ownership and/or community control of the land, whether through donation, purchase, or a long-term land lease from government, and then developing housing that will be permanently affordable. While CLT organizations retain ownership of the land, ownership of the building is retained by the CLT and leased to a nonprofit organization to provide affordable housing, or the building is owned directly by the nonprofit organization. Unlike sector-based CLTs, however, which view land ownership primarily as a legal tool to ensure affordable housing provision, the community-based organizations tend to have a broader agenda where community ownership of land is seen as the means to exercise broader community control over local development. They also engage in participatory democracy practices to fight against detrimental land uses and harmful real estate development decisions.

> The CLT is not only used for land preservation and housing provision, but also for planning and preserving socially just communities.

In urban areas like Toronto's Parkdale and Kensington Market neighbourhoods, Hamilton's Beasley neighbourhood, and the Heatherington area of Ottawa, where there is a long-standing working class, racialized, immigrant and socially progressive identity, gentrification threatens not only housing affordability, but collective social infrastructures, the local economy, and neighbourhood culture. In Vancouver's Hogan's Alley Society, the CLT acts as a way to redress the historical displacement of Vancouver's Black population. The CLT model provides a platform in such places for encouraging resident empowerment and participation and for exercising community control over neighbourhood change. In these contexts, the CLT is not only used for land preservation and housing provision, but also for planning and preserving more socially just communities.

Recent community-led CLTs have gone beyond a first-generation focus on the acquisition of land and the development of housing to engage more broadly in neighbourhood and city-wide activism, social rights advocacy, and community-led planning.

Parkdale Neighbourhood Land Trust (Toronto). The first of these second-generation, community-led CLTs to emerge was the Parkdale Neighbourhood Land Trust (PNLT). Established in 2014, the PNLT was initiated by residents and representatives from local nonprofit organizations who were concerned about the increasing gentrification of an historically working-class community. The intended role of the land trust was the acquisition and preservation of important community assets, removing them from the speculative market. A secondary goal was to enable increased democratic participation by neighbourhood residents in planning around land use. Although still in its start-up phase, PNLT has already generated strong local support. By mid 2019, it had attracted over 700 registered members and had completed two acquisitions, including an urban agricultural project and a rooming house preservation pilot project, which it intends to expand to build a portfolio of community-owned rooming houses.

Canada's charity law is more restrictive and burdensome than the 501(c)(3) designation in the United States. As a result, to accomplish its goals, Parkdale has developed a unique dual organizational model, consisting of a charity and a nonprofit that work together, but have different strategic purposes. The charitable land trust, called the Neighbourhood Land Trust (NLT), can benefit from charitable donations of land and money, but may only hold land that is used for charitable purposes and may only lease land to other charities. The charity cannot own cooperative housing or undertake community planning, both of which are not considered charitable purposes. It is also very limited in its ability to undertake political activity. The nonprofit land trust, the Parkdale Neighbourhood Land Trust (PNLT), has limited ability to fundraise, but can own and lease land more freely and has no limits on its political activity. The nonprofit land trust has a broad-based membership and community-elected board, while retaining control over the charity.

Inspired by CLTs in the United States, such as Dudley Neighbors Inc. in Boston and the Oakland CLT in the San Francisco Bay Area, PNLT has embraced the governance model of the "classic" CLT. Emphasizing community control of the organization itself, the PNLT's 15-person board of directors is elected from its resident membership. Furthermore, a tripartite board structure ensures equal representation from: "core members" who live or work on the trust's land; "organizational members" who are drawn from organizations that serve or embody the diversity of Parkdale; and "community members" who live or work within the geographic boundaries of Parkdale.

PNLT focuses its acquisition planning efforts on affordable housing and also space for community economic development, such as urban agriculture, social enterprises, and community services. With an interest in being responsive to community needs and

Fig. 3.2. PNLT members celebrating acquisition of at-risk rooming house, Toronto.

visions, the trust sets its priorities through community planning and action research. In 2016, PNLT co-led a participatory planning process, engaging 31 local organizations and over 400 residents in the creation of the *Parkdale Community Planning Study—A plan for decent work, shared wealth and equitable development in Parkdale.* The study identified an opportunity for the Neighborhood Land Trust to secure its first piece of land, a 7000 square-foot vacant property, which was acquired in 2017 through a below-market private purchase. The trust does not operate programs on the land it owns, but provides affordable land leases to eligible operating partners. Its first acquisition, now named the Milky Way Garden, is leased to Greenest City, a local environmental charity that will redevelop this vacant lot into an urban agriculture space to enhance affordable and equitable access to healthy food for local community members.

In 2017, the PNLT undertook a Community Action Research study of rooming house loss; a neighbourhood crisis that was quickly decreasing affordable single rooms and small rental units through the rapid conversion of rooming houses into upscaled rental housing or single-family homes. In response, the PNLT recruited four community organizations to implement a multi-partner Rooming House Preservation Strategy targeted to 59 at-risk rooming houses in Parkdale. Pursuing this strategy, after eight unsuccessful attempts, the Neighbourhood Land Trust has recently implemented a rooming housing preservation pilot, acquiring a 15-unit at-risk rooming house with capital funding provided by the City of Toronto. It is important to note that it was necessary to undertake two years of targeted advocacy and activism in order to build political support at the City of Toronto to make capital funding available to the land trust.[7] This funding enables and requires NLT to maintain rents at or below 80% of Average Market Rent (AMR) for a 99-year affordability period. Eligible tenants can also benefit from deeper levels of affordability, however, through rental supplements. The property will be held by the charitable NLT, but leased and operated by PARC, a local supportive housing organization.

The asset bases of PNLT and NLT are not large. Nevertheless, their public advocacy and higher profile in the press have contributed greatly to the growing public awareness and interest in CLTs, both in Toronto and across Canada.

Hamilton Community Land Trust (Ontario). The Hamilton Community Land Trust (HCLT) was formed in 2014 in the Beasley neighbourhood of Hamilton, Ontario by residents and community-based organizations who saw the need for greater community control over land use and the revitalization of Central Hamilton. This historically working-class city has long suffered from economic decline, environmental contamination, and high vacancy rates, but by 2014 a new phase of real estate reinvestment and gentrification was well underway. Between 2012 and 2015, housing prices in Hamilton rose significantly. HCLT's mandate is to hold and to steward land, acquired primarily from the municipality, and to facilitate the land's use for affordable housing or other community needs. The CLT is playing a facilitative role in the development of its lands, rather than that of a developer or operator, by working with resident groups, housing developers, and other organizations to transform underutilized properties into high-quality affordable housing, gardens, and community spaces. In 2017, HCLT acquired its first parcel of land from the City of Hamilton and then partnered with Habitat for Humanity Hamilton to develop a four-bedroom home that is being leased to a lower-income family. This initial project has demonstrated the capacity of HCLT to act as a viable organizational vehicle for redeveloping vacant city land (Hamilton Community Land Trust, 2019).

Kensington Market Community Land Trust (Toronto). Kensington Market Community Land Trust (KMCLT) was initiated in 2017 by an activist-minded group of residents who had successfully mobilized to stop the development of a WalMart store near an entrance road to the neighbourhood. The group aims to utilize the CLT to protect neighbourhood affordability more generally. Dominique Russell of KMCLT states that, "The fundamental underpinning characteristic of Kensington Market is its affordability, and we want to ensure this is preserved into the future" (Russell Interview, 2019). In recent years, Kensington Market has experienced increasing condominium development around the edges of the neighbourhood, rising rents, and "renovictions" linked to a surge in residential rehabilitation and the proliferation of short-term rentals such as AirBnB in the area. For long-term tenants and small independent store owners in this historically immigrant community, there is a shared interest in finding a way to remain in the neighbourhood and to protect its unique character (Ibid.).

KMCLT is planning to utilize the CLT for community ownership of land and community control over whatever is built upon it. The organization hopes to acquire and to preserve at-risk rental housing and storefronts. Potentially it may also oversee the redevelopment of a large municipal parking lot into a new affordable housing building. While KMCLT is still in its start-up phase of CLT development, its early success has generated support from local residents and representatives of the municipal government.

Hogan's Alley Society (Vancouver). Fifty years ago, after decades of displacement pressure on the community, the construction of the Georgia and Dunsmuir viaducts displaced an area historically known as Hogan's Alley, home to the city's Black population (Hogan's Alley Society, n.d.). In recent years, the City of Vancouver has focused efforts on removing the viaducts and is planning to revitalize the area through the North East False Creek (NEFC) area plan, approved in 2018. The Hogan's Alley Society was formed as a community-led nonprofit organization in 2017 to seek redress for the displacement of the Black community by fostering social, political, cultural and economic justice for Vancouver's Black community. Through a proposal for a nonprofit community land trust, the Hogan's Alley Society seeks to steward the land and to oversee the development of affordable housing, cultural amenities, social enterprise, and small business spaces, managing these assets in perpetuity. Negotiations with the City of Vancouver are also underway for a transfer of the former Hogan's Alley site into the CLT, a commitment made in the NEFC policy by the City Council in 2018. The redevelopment and stewardship of these lands will be led by the Hogan's Alley Society, working with partners and stakeholders in applying the CLT model to support renter households (Hogan's Alley Society, n.d.).

Sector-Based Community Land Trusts

While community-led CLTs have generated new interest in the CLT as a model for bottom-up development, sector-based CLTs have continued to demonstrate that the CLT is an effective vehicle for the development and stewardship of large stocks of affordable housing. Some first-generation CLTs, such as Colandco, have halted their housing development activities and now focus purely on the stewardship of their assets. Others are forging new growth plans. The recent formation of the Vancouver Community Land Trust Foundation (VCLTF) and HomeSpace (formerly the Calgary Community Land Trust) underscore a new phase of sector-based CLT development led by organizations with expansionist business approaches. As a result, these two sector-based CLTs are building thousands of units of new affordable housing on community-owned land and, in the process, are creating broader public recognition of the CLT model in Canada.

The Community Land Trust (Vancouver). The most prolific sector-based CLT development to be undertaken in the past decade has been led by the Cooperative Housing Federation of British Columbia (CHFBC), which controls three CLTs in the wider Vancouver area, collectively branded as *The Community Land Trust.* This recent development has occurred in the context of Vancouver's expensive housing market which, in turn, has sparked a renewed interest in cooperative and nonprofit affordable housing provision. The success of the three Vancouver-area land trusts was facilitated by enabling policy and political will at both the provincial and municipal levels. In this light, the CHFBC has imagined the CLT as a development and asset management vehicle that can deliver and steward affordable housing in direct partnership with government and the broader community housing sector.

Following in the footsteps of Colandco in Toronto, CHFBC created the Community Housing Land Trust Foundation in 1993 to hold the land and buildings of multiple cooperatives. In its early years, the Foundation acquired six properties, containing 354 units, transferred from the provincial government. The Foundation retained ownership of the land and the buildings, executing leases for the land and buildings with the independent housing cooperatives.

In 2012, a unique opportunity emerged for the CHFBC to establish a second land trust, the Vancouver Community Land Trust Foundation (VCLTF), when it won a bid competition to develop four parcels of land that were owned by the City of Vancouver. That year, CHFBC re-envisioned its model and began to self-identify as a community land trust, even rebranding its multiple land trust efforts as "The Community Land Trust." This re-framing was partially political: emphasizing the nonprofit ownership and stewardship of the land and buildings in contrast to the private provision of affordable housing that was being proposed by other developers who were competing for access to public land. It also signaled that the CLT would serve the broader community housing sector, including nonprofit and Indigenous organizations, rather than serving only cooperatives.

VCLTF has since successfully developed 358 affordable housing units on these four parcels of land. While title to the land has been retained by the City of Vancouver, the CLT has a 99-year leasehold for the land and owns the buildings until the end of the lease, when all of the improvements will revert to the City. VCLTF hopes that, at the end of this lease period, the CLT and the City will work together to redevelop the property for purposes that are consistent with their respective missions (Interview with Tom Armstrong, July 21, 2019).

Three of these properties are owned by the Community Land Trust and operated as rental housing, managed through operating agreements with three different nonprofit housing organizations. The fourth property is operated by a housing cooperative. Since the housing is operated by other organizations, the VCLTF is free to focus on other

> The Vancouver CLT Foundation has become a preferred partner for doing residential development on municipally owned land.

aspects of development and stewardship. Across its entire portfolio, tenants pay rents that range from a shelter rate to 90% of Average Market Rent. Building on this successful partnership with the City of Vancouver, VCLTF won another competitive bid in 2018 to develop an additional 1000 new affordable rental units on seven parcels of City-owned land.

While CLTs in Canada have historically faced challenges in increasing their scale, VCLTF has addressed this issue by forging strong partnerships with municipalities and by maximizing the benefits of a portfolio approach to development and stewardship; that is, when planning for new developments, VCLTF utilizes revenues generated from more profitable properties to cross-subsidize less profitable properties. This has allowed VCLTF to develop properties which may not have otherwise been financially viable. VCLTF's ability to develop affordable housing on a wide range of properties has positioned it as a preferred partner by the City of Vancouver for doing residential development on municipally owned land.

Significantly, through its multiple land trusts, CHFBC has departed from the standard practice of CLTs in other countries and has occasionally chosen to encumber its landholdings with debt, thereby "unlocking" the equity to leverage the financing needed for the development of new affordable housing. As Tiffany Duzzita, VCLTF's Director, notes:

> [T]he community land trust is a vehicle for keeping the affordable housing sector growing, and it comes down to benefits derived from the separation of land and buildings. The land component stays with the land trust, removing it from the speculative market and rising real estate costs. But the nonprofit land trust can actually use the land value as equity to redevelop and build new housing by borrowing against it. Since the land trust is mission based—it uses its (growing equity) to build more housing, not generate profit (Presentation by Tiffany Duzzita, 2017).

The community land trust has also proven to be a successful conduit through which to stabilize, improve, and redevelop existing cooperative housing assets. Recently, VCLTF took ownership of 94 cooperative homes in Abbotsford BC after the co-op experienced financial challenges. VCLTF worked with co-op members to design a comprehensive renovation plan that was funded through refinancing their existing mortgages. By bringing the co-op's assets into the land trust, the co-op benefited from an increased asset management capacity. Additionally, VCLTF provided a guarantee that the land would be protected for affordable housing on a long-term basis. Tiffany Duzzita estimates that in twelve years, the land trust will be able to leverage the increased value in the land to fund the development of an estimated 200 new units of affordable housing at the Abbotsford site, requiring little to no government assistance (Presentation by Duzzita, 2017).

HomeSpace (Calgary). The initial vision for Calgary's HomeSpace, in its previous incarnation as the Calgary Community Land Trust, was to focus on receiving cash and land donations for affordable housing, but not to develop or to operate the housing itself. HomeSpace now identifies as a nonprofit real estate corporation that seeks to provide development, property management, and asset management capacity to the affordable housing sector through the land trust model. As of early 2019, HomeSpace owned 27 buildings with a total of 520 rental units, and had an additional 211 units under development. Utilizing a partnership model, HomeSpace retains ownership of the buildings it develops and provides property management, while 17 agency partners provide support services to residents with the intention of serving diverse populations. Rents are offered at a "break-even" rate that is 20%–40% below market, with many tenants receiving deeper levels of affordability through housing allowances. One characteristic that sets Home-Space apart from many other CLTs is that it explicitly focuses on developing properties for supportive housing. It is also distinctive in not separating the ownership of land and buildings. HomeSpace continues to own both.

Over several years, HomeSpace has increased its capacity to become one of the largest nonprofit housing developers in Calgary. In 2018, HomeSpace won competitive bids to build affordable housing on three parcels of land that were owned by the City of Calgary. HomeSpace attributes its recent success and growth in part to the high level of coordination of affordable housing efforts in Calgary. The Calgary Homeless Foundation acts as the systems planner, working with local agencies and government to identify areas of greatest need, while HomeSpace acts as the nonprofit developer in partnership with government and specialized housing providers to develop projects and to serve as their long-term steward after they are built (HomeSpace Society, 2018).

CANADIAN NETWORK OF CLTs

There are currently twenty active CLTs in Canada, half of which were initiated since 2014. This recent surge in CLT development in Canada coalesced in July 2017 with the establishment of the Canadian Network of CLTs (CNCLT).[8] This new Network aims to unite both newer, community-led CLTs and more established CLTs into a cohesive, nation-wide movement. Initial objectives of the Canadian Network of CLTs include: (1) increasing government recognition of the CLT model through legislative advocacy; (2) increasing peer-to-peer resource sharing and capacity building; and (3) centering of social justice in CLT development.

In 2019, over 30 members of the fledgling Network met in person in Canada for the first time at a conference hosted by Communaute Milton-Parc in Montreal, entitled *From The Ground Up: Community Control of Land, Housing and the Economy.*

The Canadian CLT Network (*www.communityland.ca*) is still new and remains fairly ad hoc in its organization, but it has already increased collaboration and resource sharing among Canadian CLTs. If the Network can successfully facilitate cross-pollination and capacity building between community-led approaches and sector-based CLT approaches, the expectation is that Canadian CLTs will continue to grow as necessary structures for more socially just planning and affordable housing provision, while also having a greater impact on public policies.

~

CONCLUSION

The recent growth of CLTs in Canada builds upon several decades of organizing, from the 1980s onwards. In the context of large-scale government cutbacks in funding for social housing programs, social services, and community programs over the past several decades, Canadian CLTs have emerged as a relatively small, yet effective vehicle for meeting community needs and broader public priorities for affordable housing.

The "first generation" of CLTs that emerged in the 1980s were either large, sector-based organizations that prioritized affordable housing provision across cities and urban regions through partnerships with co-op housing societies, or neighbourhood-oriented and focused on community-based development through local affordable housing provision. This difference is evident in the organizational development of Colandco over the past several decades and its use of a land trust arrangement to include a portfolio of individual cooperative housing communities across Toronto. In contrast, the West Broadway CLT in Winnipeg chose to remain neighbourhood-focused, concentrating on the renovation of rent-to-own housing and supporting local community development efforts. Several of the CLTs in this first phase of Canadian CLT development created their own variations on the American CLT model, informed by the Canadian adoption of cooperatives, as a way to create affordable communities.

After 2012, the emergence of a "second generation" of CLTs followed a similar pattern of being either sector-based and expansionist in their approach to affordable housing provision or community-led and neighbourhood-based. The growth of CLTs during this period, especially over the last several years, has reflected the influence of local activists advocating for the particular needs of their surrounding community. This is evident in CLT initiatives that more broadly address the impact of gentrification, such as in Parkdale, Hamilton, and Hogan's Alley. Sector-led CLTs, on the other hand, such as the Vancouver Community Land Trust and HomeSpace, demonstrate innovative strategies to accrue land and to act as affordable housing developers through the formation of multi-sectoral partnerships and sophisticated management of their housing portfolios. With a city-wide service area, these sector-based CLTs are expanding affordable housing supply and, at the same time, increasing public awareness about the potential productivity and viability of the CLT model.

The recent establishment of a Canadian Network of CLTs, bringing together sector-based and community-based CLTs in a formal network for resource sharing and knowledge mobilization, points to a new phase of CLT development in Canada. CLT organizations are now actively engaged in creating links with one another and with organizations and networks in other countries. There has also been, of late, a much-needed discussion about Indigenous land rights and national reconciliation in relation to CLTs. Building on several decades of organizational development and advocacy, Canadian CLTs are now creating a new wave of innovative practices and opportunities for affordable housing provision and community-led development.

Notes

1. A National Housing Strategy for Canada, the first federal government initiative for affordable housing in several decades, was announced by the Liberal government in their 2016 budget. This Strategy is a 10-year, $40 billion plan to address homelessness and to subsidize the production of 100,000 new affordable housing units (National Housing Strategy, 2018).

2. 96% of all housing in Canada is currently built by the private sector (Cheung, 2017).

3. Throughout this chapter we use the term "sector-based" to refer to the nonprofit housing sector. This is a common colloquial term used by affordable housing advocates in Canada.

4. This $2 million seed grant was provided by the Campeau Corporation, a Canadan-based commercial and residential real estate development firm (Canada Mortgage and Housing Corporation, 2005).

5. The renovation of these buildings and other infrastructure was publicly funded at an estimated cost of $30 million (CAD), provided by the Canadian Mortgage and Housing Corporation, the City of Montreal, and the provincial government of Quebec (World Habitat, 2017).

6. In Canada, legislation for local level (municipal) governance is produced and enacted by provincial or territorial governments. There are ten provincial governments and three territorial governments.

7. Because of this project, the City of Toronto piloted a new approach to distributing capital funding through a fast-tracked approval process that enabled PNLT to act quickly to acquire the property on the open market.

8. The first meetings were held online with support from Grounded Solutions Network in the United States. They included representatives from Parkdale Neighbourhood Land Trust, Kensington Market CLT, Circle CLT, Colandco, Hamilton CLT, Vivacité (Montreal), Hogan's Alley, Communaute Milton-Parc, Vancouver's Community Land Trust, the North End Halifax CLT (Nova Scotia), and Heatherington Land Trust (Ottawa).

References

August, M. & Walks, A. (2018). "Gentrification, Suburban Decline, and the Financialization of Multi-Family Rental Housing: The Case of Toronto." *Geoforum* 89, 124–136.

Beaubien, LA. & Ring, L. (2006). *Preserving Community: Examining the West Broadway Community Land Trust.* Unpublished report.

Bunce, S. (2018). *Sustainability Policy, Planning, and Gentrification in Cities.* Routledge, Abingdon.

Bunce, S., Khimani, N., Sungu-Erylimaz, Y., and Earle, E. (2013). *Urban Community Land Trusts: Experiences from Canada, the United States, and Britain.* University of Toronto, Toronto.

Calgary Homeless Foundation (2012). *Calgary Homeless Foundation 2012 Annual Report.* Calgary Homeless Foundation, Calgary.

Canada Mortgage and Housing Corporation (2005). *Critical Success Factors for Community Land Trusts in Canada: Final Report.* Canada Mortgage and Housing Corporation, Ottawa.

Canadian Cooperative Housing Federation of Toronto (2019) <*https://co-ophousingto-ronto.coop*> Last accessed: July 1, 2019.

Communitas Inc. (1985). *Land Trusts for Non-Profit Continuing Housing Co-operatives.* Cooperative Housing Federation of Canada.

Hamilton Community Land Trust (2019). <*https://www.hamiltonclt.org*> Last accessed: July 22, 2019.

Home Space Society (2018). <*https://www.homespace.org*> Last accessed: July 22, 2019.

Hogan's Alley Society (n.d.). <*http://www.hogansalleysociety.org*> Last accessed: July 22, 2019.

Hulchanski, D. (1983). "Co-operative Land Management: The Potential of Linking a Community Land Trust to Government Housing Supply Programs," Pp. 35–50 in: D. Hulchanski (Ed.) *Managing Land for Housing: The Experience of Housing Co-operatives in British Columbia.* Centre for Human Settlements, University of British Columbia.

Hulchanski, D. (1988). "The Evolution of Property Rights and Housing Tenure in Post-War Canada: Implications for Housing Policy," *Urban Law and Policy* 9, 135–156.

Interview with Brian Finley (2013). Toronto.

Interview with Tom Clement (2019). Toronto.

Interview with Dominique Russell (2019). Toronto.

Interview with Tom Armstrong (2019). Toronto.

Kowaluk, L. & Piche-Burton, C. (eds.)(2012). *Communaute Milton-Parc: How We Did It and How It Works Now.* Communaute Milton-Parc, Montreal.

La Communaute Milton Parc (2013). <*http://www.miltonparc.org/about-us/*> Last accessed: July 22, 2019.

Presentation by Tiffany Duzzita (2017). ONPHA Conference, Niagara Falls.

Roussopoulos, Dimitrios and Hawley, Josh (eds.)(2018). *Villages in Cities: Community Land Ownership, Cooperative Housing, and the Milton Parc Story.* Montreal: Black Rose Books.

Vernon and District Community Land Trust Society (2012). <*http://www.communityland. ca/canadian-clts/*> Last accessed: July 22, 2019.

Walks, A. (2014). "From Financialization to Socio-Spatial Polarization of the City: Evidence from Canada," *Economic Geography* 90(1), 33–66.

World Habitat (2017). Milton Parc Community <*https://www.world-habitat.org/world-habitat-awards/winners-and-finalists/milton-park-community/*> Last accessed: July 22, 2019.

4.

Stewardship of Urban Real Estate for Long-Term Community Benefit
Profile of the Urban Land Conservancy in Denver, Colorado

Alan Gottlieb and Aaron Miripol

The Urban Land Conservancy (ULC) was established in 2003 as a nonprofit corporation with a service area encompassing the Denver metropolitan area. Since then, ULC has grown and evolved to the point that it is now a major player in Denver's real estate scene. Its influence extends beyond the number of acres it owns and the number of developments it has sponsored. An integral part of both its internal success and its wider influence also comes from the organization's early adoption of key features of the community land trust (CLT).

ULC is not a traditional CLT. It actively involves community residents in planning its developments, but ULC does not have a community-based membership that elects a majority of its governing board. Unlike most CLTs in the United States, moreover, ULC's development of affordable housing has not included homeownership. Nevertheless, by any other measure, ULC has exemplified and championed the CLT model to a degree that few organizations have matched. ULC owns land in perpetuity. It strategically uses 99-year ground leases to preserve prime pieces of land in multiple neighborhoods facing the pressures of gentrification, ensuring the availability of those lands for the lasting benefit of low-income people in a booming real estate market. Its ground leases provide ULC with a legal mechanism for ensuring the permanent affordability of its place-based investments in multi-family rental housing and nonprofit facilities.

ULC is a unique organization with a singular history. We will review the organization's origins and describe the major projects that ULC has developed using the CLT model. We will also examine how ULC emphasizes and involves community, even though ULC's organizational structure differs significantly from that of a traditional CLT. Finally, we will consider what the future holds for CLT development in Metro Denver, as ULC incubates the Elevation CLT, a new organization that will be structured and operated along lines of the "classic" community land trust.

FROM IDEA TO EXECUTION

It was 2003 when the pieces of a puzzle snapped into place for Denver oilman Sam Gary. A philanthropist who had founded the Piton Foundation as well the Gary-Williams Energy Corporation, Gary had long admired how nonprofits like the Trust for Public Land and Colorado Open Lands acquired land in beautiful places to ensure the parcels would always provide a public benefit.

Why, he wondered, couldn't something similar be done with land in cities where real estate costs are rapidly escalating? Shouldn't there be a way to acquire urban land to ensure that any investment in the preservation of existing buildings or the development of new buildings would accrue as a lasting benefit to the public? In Gary's words:

> I developed my understanding of the value of land conservation early on, in the open lands conservation movement. I broadened my focus from open lands to urban lands. That sensibility converged with my desire to strengthen our urban communities where our most underserved children and families live.

As the funder of a philanthropic foundation, Gary had also grown frustrated with the struggles of nonprofits to buy buildings for the purpose of housing their own operations, only to see those properties occasionally lost to bank foreclosure when a nonprofit organization hit financial difficulties down the road.

After Sam Gary's epiphany, the leadership of his charitable foundation and his energy company began working together to flesh out his idea of creating a structure for acquiring and holding urban land for public benefit. Initially, Gary favored creating a land bank inside the Piton Foundation. But over time, he was persuaded that something more robust was needed. He realized, according to his nephew, Tim Howard, that "starting an organization that had a good mission and a sustainable operating model was a better way to go than creating a new program area within a small private foundation."

Tim Howard, despite his employment on the oil exploration side of the Gary-Williams Energy Corporation, had an abiding interest in helping Gary to create a land bank inside the Piton Foundation. He was given the assignment of putting together a plan for the nascent ULC and running the organization while a board was being put together and as ULC was getting off the ground.

"You can imagine a line of army recruits standing there," wryly commented Howard years later. "The drill sergeant says, 'all volunteers take one step forward,' and everyone takes one steps back except one guy who didn't quite hear the instructions. I was that guy."

Howard was a quick study, but he had no background in community development. Thanks to the deep connections within Denver's real estate community that Gary and his staff had formed over decades of philanthropic endeavors, however, ULC was able to assemble a powerhouse board of real estate developers, finance experts, and local philanthropists to oversee its operations, even before the organization officially existed.

The board's first chair was Tom Gougeon, who in the 1980s had served as a senior aide to Denver Mayor Federico Peña. He went on to head the Stapleton Redevelopment Foundation, leading the planning for what would be built on the massive site of Denver's old airport. He later became a private real estate developer, which was his role when he took the helm of the ULC board. He currently serves as president of the Gates Family Foundation in Denver. He recalls:

> We starting thinking about whether there was room for a land trust equivalent focused on the urban marketplace. It was a broader and different idea than the CLT model. It was more than housing. It was really this all-purpose real estate agent that could go out and intervene in the marketplace on behalf of the community. We were interested in schools and nonprofit space, health, and parks.

Conversations ensued with the Denver Foundation, a local community foundation, which adopted ULC as a "supporting organization" and provided ULC with administrative and accounting services during its first decade, while managing ULC's cash as a donor-advised fund. The Foundation also appointed half the members of ULC's board, a practice that has continued to the present. Otherwise the Foundation does not intervene in ULC's development decisions or in its day-to-day operations.

ULC GROWS UP

In its early years, with no staff, ULC operated in an opportunistic fashion, pursuing attractive real estate deals as they became available. Susan Powers, a Denver-based developer and former head of the Denver Urban Renewal Authority who served on the inaugural ULC board, recalled developing with Tom Gougeon and with other members of the board a list of projects they'd like to pursue.

The new organization got a major boost in 2007, when the Gary-Williams Energy Corporation donated three properties to ULC, together valued at more than $7 million. This included the Tramway Building, occupying a square block in the low-income Cole neighborhood, and a former Budget Motel in northeast Denver, leased to the Colorado Coalition for the Homeless serving families coming out of homelessness. The Corporation also endowed ULC with a donation of cash to leverage other real estate purchases. There were no written restrictions placed on how the money could be used. Susan Powers later recalled the feeling of amazement that came over them in that moment:

> Then one day Sam Gary said he wanted to have a phone call with me and Tom, and on that call he told us he wanted to give us $10 million. Obviously, it was extremely generous, and it meant that we weren't going to be a land conservancy starting from scratch. But it did make us wonder how we were going to do this as a group of volunteers.

Gary's largess prompted ULC's board to decide that the time had come to hire a full-time president & chief executive officer. The board launched a national search. Several board members were already familiar with Aaron Miripol or knew him by reputation. Miripol had been running Thistle Community Housing in Boulder County since 1998. Thistle was a community development corporation that had established, developed, and administered a successful CLT as an internal program, one of only two CLTs in Colorado at the time.

Miripol, a CLT expert and an evangelist for the model, had impressed Sam Gary, Tim Howard and others from Gary-Williams and the Piton Foundation during an earlier trip they had taken to Boulder to learn about Thistle's CLT. "Aaron gets a lot of credit for really pushing forward the CLT concept. So when it came time to hire a leader for ULC, he was the first person I thought of," Howard said.

The rest of the board agreed. Miripol took the helm of the ULC in mid-2007. In Howard's estimation, time has proven the wisdom of the board's choice:

> ULC would be another one of those nonprofits that the foundation community tried to start and get off the ground but somehow wasn't sustainable if Aaron hadn't taken that job. The key is the overlap between his belief in and understanding of permanent stewardship through the CLT and all the different manifestations it has to take to adapt to different community needs. That and the fact that he is like an energizer bunny. His go-go ability to get stuff done and motivate people, whether partners or his staff, is a unique thing that has allowed ULC to succeed.

COMMUNITY LAND TRUST PROJECTS, 2007–2019

After being hired by ULC, Miripol's first task was to build the organization's internal capacity to manage the properties donated by Sam Gary and to begin planning and developing large-scale projects. In the ensuing years, ULC has gone from a staff of one to a staff of 17 full-time employees.

One of Miripol's enduring contributions to ULC has been his ability to attract and hire high-quality staff, with both knowledge of the development field and passion for the work. It's the strength of the staff from top to bottom that provides ULC with sufficient capacity to do such a high volume of excellent work. The extraordinarily strong, committed staff makes ULC a true, mission-driven organization.

By 2019, the organization had overseen the development of eight major projects using the CLT model, representing a total investment of $37 million in equity. Five of these CLT projects are described below. They provide insight into the diversity of ULC's activities and the versatility of doing equitable and sustainable development on community-owned land.

Jody Apartments, Housing Preservation Near Public Transit

ULC's first CLT investment was the $725,000 purchase in 2007 of two acres of land under Jody Apartments, an existing 62-unit rental housing complex serving lower-income households located on Denver's western border. These apartments are next to a stop on the light rail line of the Regional Transportation District (RTD), connecting downtown Denver to the western suburb of Golden.

NEWSED, a community development corporation that has operated in Denver since 1973, had wanted to buy the property with the intention of rehabilitating the four buildings and preserving them as affordable housing. NEWSED initially approached ULC to ask about receiving a construction loan. ULC declined. Instead, hewing to its mission, ULC used its investment to buy the land underneath Jody Apartments, while NEWSED continued to own and to manage these buildings as rental housing.

NEWSED leases the land from ULC through a 99-year ground lease. Under the terms of the ground lease, 52 of the 62 apartments must remain permanently affordable. Twelve of the 52 are reserved for extremely low-income households (families earning $20,000 or less per year).

More recently, ULC acquired four additional acres adjacent to both Jody Apartments and the light rail station, thereby maximizing the opportunity to provide permanently affordable housing and nonprofit facilities at the site. Development is underway on the first phase. ULC is partnering with two for-profit affordable housing developers, Brinshore Development and Mile High, in building Sheridan Station Residences, 133 permanently affordable apartments atop a 99-year ground lease with ULC. Ultimately, the balance of the four-acre site will provide 250 additional affordable homes, along with up to 50,000 feet of commercial space.

Holly Square Shopping Center

ULC's highest-profile and most impactful CLT investment to date has been the redevelopment of the Holly Square shopping center in the historically African-American neighborhood of Northeast Park Hill.[1] The Holly, as it is widely known, was formerly a center of Denver's African-American community, and a source of pride for many. In its heyday, from the mid-1950s to mid-1970s, the shopping center was anchored by a Safeway supermarket, and also featured a barber shop, a hardware store, a dentistry office, a general apparel store, a dry cleaner, a variety store and a candy store, among other small businesses. Many of these enterprises were owned by African-Americans.

When the supermarket closed in the mid 1970s, The Holly began to deteriorate. Its anchor space remained vacant for several years until the Hope Center, a local nonprofit, purchased the supermarket for its home in 1979. Then, in the late 1980s, on the heels of the crack cocaine epidemic that swept the nation, local affiliates of Los Angeles street gangs arrived on the scene. A newspaper article described The Holly of the late 1980s as "home base for the Park Hill Bloods."

The center hit its nadir in May 2008, when a rival gang firebombed The Holly in retaliation for the fatal shooting of one of its leaders. The burned-out center could have become a blighted eyesore, casting a pall over the surrounding area. Instead, community leaders vowed to replace it with something better.

After city officials initiated conversations about The Holly's future with Aaron Miripol, ULC bought the 2.6-acre property for $625,000, part of which was covered by a $200,000 forgivable loan from the City of Denver. Working together, community residents, city officials, the Denver Foundation, and ULC created a participatory community-planning process known as the Holly Area Redevelopment Project (HARP).

Members of the HARP steering committee gathered input from neighborhood residents about the kinds of services, programs, and businesses that should occupy the space.[2] What ultimately resulted was a plan for the complete transformation of Holly Square, anchored by a new Boys & Girls Club and a public elementary school, housed within new buildings that sit atop land that is owned by ULC.

The Boys & Girls Club has a 99-year land lease with ULC, which will automatically renew for another 99 years. The Boys & Girls Club paid ULC for development rights that were 75 percent below market-rate with annual land-lease payments to ULC of less than $5,000 per year. The development fee paid off ULC's debt on the land and a portion of its holding costs.

Fig. 4.1. The new Boys & Girls Club at Holly Square.

Unfortunately, the Roots Elementary School closed in 2019 due to low enrollment, caused in part by poor educational performance. However, because ULC still owns the land under the Roots building, ULC is leading the negotiations with interested non-profits who want to call the Holly their home.

The shopping center also has an adjacent public library and city recreation center, making it a true hub of the community. The former head of Roots Elementary called The Holly a "mini Harlem Children's Zone." Thanks to the land leases, both the Boys & Girls

Club and the former school facilities will remain community assets far into the future. This is a lasting community benefit, described by Miripol as follows:

> We want to be good stewards of the Holly property, and one way of doing that is protecting the future use through our CLT 99-year ground leases. When you combine what HARP has done with all of the positive changes taking place at Dahlia (another recently redeveloped shopping center in the neighborhood), you have a number of impactful assets, all of them important pieces of a vibrant community.

Curtis Park Community Center

ULC purchased the vacant Curtis Park Community Center in 2012 for $600,000 from the American Baptist Church of the Rocky Mountain Region. The purchase price was partially offset by a $350,000 forgivable loan from the City of Denver. The center is located in the heart of the Curtis Park neighborhood, a rapidly gentrifying area filled with stately Victorian homes.

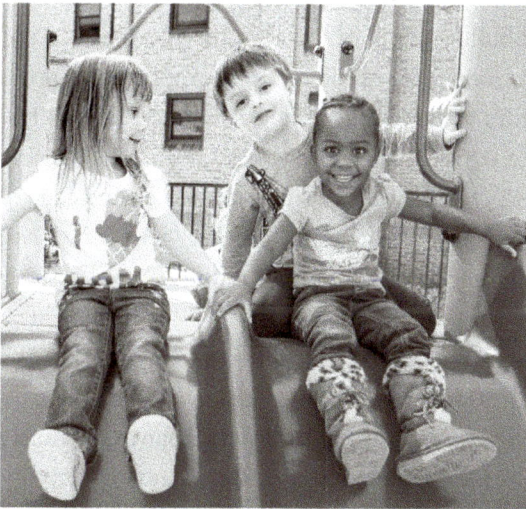

Fig. 4.2. Playground, Family Star Montessori.

ULC entered into an agreement to revitalize the site with a venerable early childhood program, Family Star Montessori, which serves children from low-income families. ULC partnered with Family Star in completing $1.2 million in renovations that were needed to open the school. In 2017, Family Star bought the renovated building from ULC for $885,000, with a 99-year ground lease for the underlying land. Family Star makes annual lease payments of $7,000 to help compensate ULC for the roughly $750,000 that ULC "left in the land." These lease payments provide ULC with a one percent return on its investment in the land. ULC plays a unique role in not only ensuring the nonprofit's beneficial use of the property, but also providing opportunities for mission-driven organizations to become anchors in their communities.

New Legacy Charter School

The New Legacy Charter School Project provides another example of how land ownership has allowed ULC to preserve and, in this case, to create important community assets. New Legacy is a small charter high school designed to serve teen parents and their children. The school is home to a fully licensed infant-through-early-childhood center, so that teen parents can attend classes knowing their children are close at hand and safe in an enriching environment.

Before the school existed, its founder approached ULC for help in finding a facility in NW Aurora, a low-income section of Denver's largest inner-ring suburb. After a few failed attempts to secure a facility, ULC purchased a vacant bowling alley in 2014 for $675,000 with plans to convert it to a school. Ultimately, ULC and New Legacy decided that a better solution would be to demolish the building and to start fresh. The result was a new, gleaming 23,000 square-foot school building that opened in the fall of 2015. It was made possible by the creative financing assembled by ULC.

After protracted negotiations, the school and ULC agreed on a formula for determining rent payments for the building. Under the terms of the lease, New Legacy has an option to purchase the building from ULC upon expiration of the original five-year agreement (in 2020). Should the school eventually buy the building, ULC will retain ownership of the land, conveying the site to the school through a renewable 99-year ground lease.

The Site at 38th and Blake Streets

In 2011, ULC purchased two abandoned buildings out of foreclosure at 38th Street and Blake Street for $1.7 million ($26/square foot), just ahead of a real estate boom in the Cole neighborhood that has seen the land's value appreciate by 500 percent. This 1.5-acre site, adjacent to the Blake Street Station on RTD's light rail line, was purchased using Denver's Transit Oriented Development (TOD) Fund. The site is located on the edge of Cole, a working-class community caught in a vise between the booming, gentrified River North neighborhood and a massive reconstruction of Interstate 70 running through central Denver.

ULC had originally envisioned developing a five-story residential building on the site, providing 114 income-restricted units. However, ULC's partner, Medici Consulting Group (MCG), was denied twice by the Colorado Housing and Finance Authority (CHFA) when it applied for tax credits for the project, due to fierce statewide competition for the credits. Following the second rejection, ULC opted to split its holdings into two parcels: 3789 Walnut Street and 3750 Blake Street. MCG then applied successfully for tax credits for the Walnut Street Lofts and ULC began working to sell the Blake Street site to another developer.

In March 2019, MCG broke ground on 66 units of permanently affordable housing at the corner of 38th and Walnut on the southeast side of the property, providing one-, two- and three-bedroom units for households earning 30%-60% of the Area Median Income. In addition, the property will join ULC's growing community land trust through the implementation of a 99-year renewable ground lease agreement to ensure the property remains affordable in perpetuity.

In selling the other parcel, ULC negotiated with a developer to include at least 30 income-restricted units, 11 more than was required by the City's zoning overlay. In addition, ULC negotiated a First Right of Refusal (at a below-market price) to purchase the

Fig. 4.3. Before and after: the site at 38th and Blake Streets when first acquired by ULC in 2011 (top); a rendering of the rental housing built on the site (bottom).

30 units if the owner were to decide in the future to convert the rental building into for-sale condos.

Together, the 3789 Walnut Street and 3750 Blake Street parcels will provide 96 permanently affordable, income-restricted apartments. The proceeds from the sale of the Blake Street lot to the developer also allowed ULC to plan for additional affordable housing four blocks away at Cole Train, next to the Tramway Nonprofit Center.

The Site at 48th Avenue and Race Street

ULC purchased a six-acre site at East 48th Avenue and Race Street in April 2015 for $5.5 million with loans from the City of Denver and the Calvert Impact Fund. The Colorado Health Foundation provided additional funding to support healthy design and development. The site is located near a new, soon-to-be-opened commuter rail station in Elyria-Swansea, a neighborhood that was cut in two in the early 1960s by the construction of Interstate 70. The area is home to a number of industrial sites and adjacent to the National Western Stock Show. The latter is being redeveloped into a year-round tourist destination. It will also provide new and improved multi-modal pathways to reconnect Elyria and Swansea, bringing life back into these communities.

In 2018, after conducting a year-long community engagement process to create designs for future development, ULC announced that Columbia Ventures LLC would be its development partner for the $150 million project on ULC's six-acre site. Plans include both permanently affordable housing and market-rate housing, as well as the construction of 50,000 square feet of community commercial space.

This development project will also provide a new home for Clinica Tepayac, a 25-year-old nonprofit health clinic providing culturally competent health services for the medically underserved. Clinica Tepayac's 25,000 square-foot facility will become part of ULC's community land trust to ensure long-term community benefit. With the recent award of federal and state tax credits,[3] 150 permanently affordable apartments will be built above Clinica's new health clinic. The eventual completion of all parts of this transit-oriented development at 48th and Race will more than quadruple the supply of permanently affordable housing in the neighborhood.

HOW ULC PUTS THE "C" IN CLT

The Urban Land Conservancy is not a typical community land trust. Many CLTs across the country are formed to work in a single neighborhood, with a sole focus on homeownership. That is not the case with the ULC, which has acquired and developed multiple properties across the Denver metropolitan area and does no homeownership. All of the housing on its lands are multi-unit rentals. As Tom Gougeon has noted:

> ULC never was going to be built on the classic homeownership land trust model: community grass-rootsy, advocacy-based organizations. This is partly because of the small geography of those organizations, compared to the ULC's geographical scope.

It is also the case that most CLTs across the country are overseen by a board with significant representation from the people who live in the CLT's properties. Because ULC has not done homeownership, it does not have the same representation. Instead, board members are chosen from the community for their expertise in development, law, finance and/or government. The complexity of the organization and the variety of its projects makes an expertise-based board a necessity. Again, according to Tom Gougeon:

> If you think about what ULC has been doing, it is a much more sophisticated operation with a broader set of skills required than even a good-sized CLT. ULC projects include housing, yes, but also office buildings and retail space and schools. They all have different financing structures and regulatory structures, and are spread across many municipalities. That is why you need a board with the attributes of ULC's board. You may not

need all of that in a traditional CLT, which leaves more room for resident representation ULC is a kindred enterprise to a CLT, but an outlier because of those factors.

Still, ULC puts significant effort into community involvement. The clearest example is the Holly Square redevelopment, where the Holly Area Redevelopment Project committee included significant community representation. HARP members chose the partners that ultimately occupied the property.

In the summer of 2018, ULC hired two "managers of neighborhood partnerships" to oversee the organization's work in communities where it owns properties. Both individuals have deep roots in Metro Denver neighborhoods, and extensive experience in community organizing.

"Hiring them was critical to building stronger relationships with community stakeholders," Miripol said. "That was an area where we hadn't had the capacity we needed." In 2018, ULC added a CLT committee to its organization. The committee consists of representatives from organizations that "own the improvements" on lands owned by ULC.

Why has it taken so long for ULC to create a CLT committee? According to Miripol, it takes a certain economy of scale to form such a committee. ULC currently has five CLT entities, with a sixth and seventh coming in the next year. In previous years, it wouldn't have made sense to form a CLT committee because there would have been few members, representing a small number of properties. But recent and upcoming growth in ULC's CLT properties made this the right time to put together a committee.

SUCCESSES AND CHALLENGES IN THE CLT REALM

From Aaron Miripol's perspective, ULC's most notable successes in the CLT realm have come when partners have understood the value to both parties of community-owned land and long-term ground leases. Conversely, the biggest challenges have arisen when there was a lack of understanding of the model used by ULC to preserve affordability and to protect community assets.

The Holly Shopping Center redevelopment is the jewel in ULC's community land trust crown. "It's a quintessential use of the CLT because stakeholders have confidence that the land will never go to market, regardless of what happens to the programs currently operating there," Miripol said. Indeed, the site will remain a hub of the community for 198 years, thanks to automatically renewing 99-year ground leases on the land under the Boys & Girls Club and the former Roots Elementary School.

In a similar vein, the Curtis Park Community Center purchase ensures long-term community benefit for a property in the heart of a neighborhood undergoing an inexorable transformation caused by gentrification. And the Jody Apartments will remain affordable in perpetuity, thanks to a long-term ground lease.

In all three cases, initial reluctance on the part of ULC's partners about entering into a ground lease rather than buying the land was overcome by the cost savings realized by not having to purchase the land.

Conversely, ULC's most challenging projects have been those where long-term ground leasing would have made sense but the projects' partners couldn't be persuaded that this approach would serve them better than owning the land. As Miripol explains:

> Even with our successes, there continues to be a lack of commitment to the use of CLTs. We have folks that struggle with the idea of ULC owning the land, as if it limits their ability to get full market rate in the future. Owning the land is a value we bring by taking the up-front risk of purchasing a property. We don't want to ever sell the land because we believe that regardless of whether you're the greatest nonprofit or for-profit developer, we don't know what a neighborhood is going to look like 20–30 years from now and what its changing needs will be.

Another challenge to expanding ULC's portfolio of community-owned land is Denver's real estate boom. Land is overpriced at the moment, making it difficult to do any kind of real estate deal, be it a CLT or something more traditional.

But it is at precisely such moments that an organization like ULC becomes so vital to maintaining the essential fabric of the community. According to Susan Powers, a private developer who served on ULC's board for a decade, "Timing is everything. ULC has to be the organization that looks well into the future and finds ways to keep projects alive when no one else can."

WHAT THE FUTURE HOLDS FOR ULC AND CLT DEVELOPMENT IN COLORADO

The Urban Land Conservancy currently owns several parcels of land where it plans to employ CLT ground leases in future developments. One is the site of a former Thriftway supermarket in a low-income neighborhood in southwest Denver that is beginning to experience gentrification. ULC bought the property in 2014, demolished the building, and contracted with a local community organizing group to solicit deep community involvement in determining how the site should be redeveloped.

In 2016, following an intensive community engagement process, ULC completed construction of an interim pocket park and futsal court on the property. Long-term plans for the site are to do beneficial development that addresses the needs of the community. Through a future community engagement process, ULC will create a catalytic neighborhood asset for Westwood residents. One thing is certain: Whatever permanent facilities are built on the site will sit on land that ULC continues to own.

In the summer of 2018, ULC received its largest donation to date with the former Excelsior Youth Campus in Aurora, a 31-acre site that includes seventeen buildings. Now called Oxford Vista, the campus is headquarters for the Southwest Division of Americorps' National Community Conservation Corps. Another nonprofit, Family Tree, is leasing four buildings on the site to provide housing, early childhood education, and other services for families coming out of homelessness. ULC's long-term expectation is that the entire campus will be in a community land trust

Finally, ULC has played a leading role in starting the Elevation Community Land Trust (ECLT). In this case, ULC is developing an organization, rather than developing or redeveloping a parcel of land. Elevation CLT is a regional CLT that focuses on affordable homeownership. It is being incubated by ULC until the program can be spun off to become its own independent, tax-exempt, not-for-profit corporation.

"Elevation will provide all of the stewardship components related to homeownership like homebuyer counseling, which are services ULC doesn't provide," said Dave Younggren, President and CEO of Gary Community Investments and the Piton Foundation, the successor organization to Gary-Williams Energy Corporation.

Rather than being concentrated in a single neighborhood — or in a single city — Elevation CLT will use a scattered-site approach and have the flexibility to go to scale in any community at risk of gentrification and displacement. Its service area will eventually

Fig. 4.4. Aerial view of the 31-acre Oxford Vista site in Aurora, Colorado.

> Elevation CLT will have the flexibility to go to scale in any community at risk of gentrification and displacement.

expand beyond Denver Metro to support CLT homeownership across Colorado. To further support low-income families in the communities it serves, the Elevation CLT aims to align itself with comprehensive supportive services programs that provide residents with increased access to health care and healthy food, early childhood education, workforce training and placement, and wealth-building opportunities.

Elevation is being launched with a $24 million investment from a consortium of local philanthropic foundations, led by Gary Community Investments. Sam Gary's original vision for land ownership has now come full circle. It has ended up right back where it started — preserving urban land for community benefit.

Since its founding in 2003, ULC has made 37 real estate investments totaling over $120 million. Through its developments, ULC has leveraged an additional $700 million for the development of affordable housing (over 1,000 homes) and nonprofit facilities (700,000 square feet). Its projects have created more than 2,000 jobs. Its impact on the Denver metro area is undeniable. As Dave Younggren has observed:

> The community land trust as implemented by ULC has worked extremely well. The organization has done a remarkable job working in our community and is widely viewed as a real community resource and asset.

Controlling the land means controlling the impact and affordability of real estate, not only in the immediate future, but for multiple generations. It is important to think about how urban real estate fits into the fabric of community. ULC has proven how a CLT can ensure a positive impact in perpetuity.

Notes

1. A full history of the project can be found here: *https://www.urbanlandc.org/wp-content/uploads/2018/06/Holly-Final-reduced.pdf*

2. Staff from the Denver Foundation's Strengthening Neighborhoods initiative did much of the legwork of recruiting members for the HARP steering committee and ensuring that it represented the community's varied voices and interests.

3. Much of the equity raised by ULC for the recent development of three multi-family CLT projects — Sheridan Station, Walnut Lofts, and 48th & Race — has come from the Low Income Housing Tax Credit (LIHTC) program. This program was created in 1986 under Section 42 of the IRS Tax Code. It is currently the largest source of federal funding for the production of affordable rental housing. More than 900 units of housing have been built on ULC's sites using this program, roughly 80% of ULC's total affordable housing production.

5.

London Community Land Trust
A Story of People, Power, and Perseverance

Dave Smith

Ponti's isn't there anymore. It was a little Italian café which hung from the rafters of Liverpool Street train station — one of London's considerably more perfunctory termini, which sits on the boundary of where the historic City of London meets what is commonly known as the East End.

Ponti's was never particularly famous for very much, although reportedly its full English breakfast and coffee wasn't all that bad. But in 1996 it did star — albeit very briefly — as the setting for a conversation between two of the leading protagonists in a new Hollywood film that was to be called *Mission: Impossible.* So it is rather apt, perhaps, that it was also here, in the late autumn of 2008, that the initial conversation about a potential site for London's first-ever community land trust project took place.

This is the story of that site — St Clements Hospital — and of the people and organisations who, over the next ten years, fought so long and so hard to turn that initial conversation at Ponti's into the permanently affordable CLT homes that stand there today. But whilst it is a good story in many ways, it lacks what is perhaps the key ingredient of any great story: namely, a definitive and happy ending. Not because there haven't been some real highs and lasting achievements within the organisation's first decade — there have been many. But because what has also emerged during this time is the sheer scale and deepening extent of the housing problem, and how desperately the CLT's work is needed. And so it is unlikely that this is a story that will come to an end any time soon.

Today, the London CLT has active campaigns relating to twelve potential further sites across the capital. Based upon its most conservative projections, the organization is now on track to deliver some 110 new permanently affordable homes by 2022. This will see upwards of 300 people living in CLT homes in parts of the city as far apart as Croydon and Redbridge; in places of such historical and cultural significance as Cable Street and Brixton; and maybe even on the Olympic Park. But with over 8,500 people sleeping rough last year, with 365,000 children under the age of 16 still living in accommodations that are legally deemed "overcrowded," and with over 240,000 households still on government waiting lists for affordable housing in one of the wealthiest cities in the world — St Clements was only ever going to be able to be considered a success if it was merely the beginning of a much longer story, laying the foundation for a CLT that could do even more in the future.

AN UNAFFORDABLE CITY — A BRIEF HISTORY

The housing crisis in London (and especially in the city's East End, where the London CLT got its start) is nothing new. Charles Booth — the great Victorian social researcher and reformer — in his famed "Poverty Maps" of 1891, described some of the neighbouring streets around what is now the St Clements site as being typified by the "Very poor, casual. Chronic want."

Where Victorian slums had dominated, post-war governments of all political colours took the opportunity afforded to them by the Luftwaffe to remake vast swathes of the East End following the annihilation of its Docklands between 1939–45. In their place were built large-scale social housing estates — concrete monoliths promising "streets in the sky." Local politicians looked to outbid each other in regards to the number of new homes they promised to build during each election cycle. This interventionist consensus, broadly speaking, remained the case until the end of the 1970s, when Horace Cutler (the Chairman of Housing and, later, Leader of the Conservative party within the Greater London Council), and then Margaret Thatcher, actively sought to curb the ability of local councils to build subsidized public housing in an attempt to reduce their political opponents' power base. The effect was that the overall number of new homes being built in London — and particularly the number of *affordable* homes being built — fell off a cliff edge: down from about 35,000 a year in total in 1969 to fewer than 14,000 a year in 1985. The private sector (thoroughly aware of the impact that a decrease in supply would have on its profitability) never picked up the slack. So prices began to rise in relation to earnings — albeit at a relatively moderate rate at first, as the great legacy of the welfare state clung on and the economic volatility of the 1980s gave way to recession in the early 1990s.

The picture changed, however, in the closing years of the Twentieth Century. With an economic recovery, coupled with the election of a New Labour government in 1997 and a belief in all things "third way," the British housing market embarked upon a record run of unbroken economic growth that would last for fifteen years. These were boom times. One of the nation's largest mortgage lenders, Northern Rock, demutualized to become a bank in the same year. It infamously offered "120% loan-to-value interest-only" mortgages to first-time homebuyers, a sign that both the bank and homebuyers were convinced that the property market would rise indefinitely. As such, borrowers were encouraged to take out a loan for more than a house's value, spend the extra capital on moving and furnishing costs, and plan to never repay the capital sum, believing all the while that they could still make money out of the property's appreciation.

House prices in London rose from an average of £96,000 in 1997 to over £300,000 just ten years later. The global economic crash of 2008 took its toll briefly, but by the summer of 2012 house prices were back to where they had previously been and quickly rose again. As of 2019, the average house price (the geometric mean) across the whole city of eight million people stood at £478,853 ($631,998). This was approximately fourteen times the average Londoner's salary of £34,000 ($44,873) and nearly twice that of the national average house price of £243,583 ($321,485) in a country that is known to have a nationwide housing crisis.

COMMUNITY ORGANIZING AROUND LONDON'S BID TO HOST THE 2012 OLYMPICS

The impact of these macro-economic trends was plain for all to see at street level. In East London, at meetings of The East London Communities Organisation (TELCO) — the country's first and now largest community organising federation, known today as Citizens UK — stories poured forth about the crippling costs of rent and a homeownership market out of reach. Following its earlier transformative success with the Living

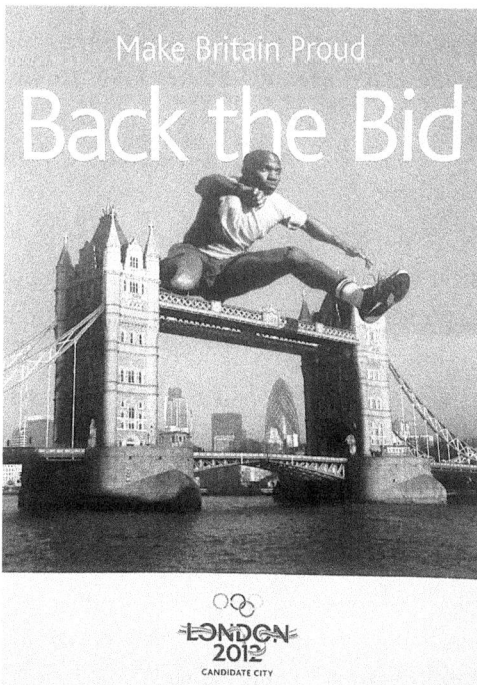

Fig. 5.1. Poster urging London's citizens to support the city's bid to host the 2012 Olympics.

Wage Campaign, Neil Jameson — TELCO's founding Executive Director, who had trained at the Industrial Areas Foundation in the late 1980s and exported Saul Alinksy's organising model to the UK — decided that housing needed to form a central plank of the organisation's new agenda. And a prime organising opportunity soon appeared in the summer of 2005, thanks to a meeting taking place some six thousand miles away in Singapore.

London had recently declared its intention to bid for host city status for the 2012 Summer Olympic Games. Sensing their chance to leverage influence within a formative political debate — and especially given the desire of the authorities to secure local support for a bid that was premised on a promise of a "legacy" of regeneration for East London, amidst an anticipated total spend of £8.7 billion — TELCO forced itself into a relationship with the London 2012 Bid Team and invited the Team to one of TELCO's public assemblies. Built on a foundation of thousands of one-to-one conversations within trades unions, churches, mosques, schools, and other civic institutions across East London, the result of the organizing effort was the preparation and public signing of an "Ethical Charter for The Games." This agreement guaranteed a defined set of community benefits in exchange for TELCO's support for the Olympic bid. Amongst them was a commitment to new jobs and the payment of a Living Wage for all staff at the Olympics. There was also a commitment to build, once the Games were over, "2012 permanently affordable homes for local people through a Community Land Trust and mutual home ownership."

The announcement by the International Olympic Committee in Singapore on July 6, 2005 that London was to be awarded the right to host the Games of the XXX Olympiad was largely unexpected and met with mixed emotions across the British capital. Paris had been widely expected to win, and many Londoners greeted the news with a combination of stereotypical British disdain and reserve, as well as newfound fears about the implications for where they would be able to park. But for those in TELCO, the mood could not have been happier. The Ethical Charter for The Games had been signed by none other than Lord Sebastien Coe, head of the Bid Team and now the Chairman of the London Organising Committee of the Olympic and Paralympic Games (LOCOG), and by the Mayor of London, Ken Livingstone. That agreement looked set to ensure that London's first CLT was a done deal and headed for rapid success in the years ahead. But sadly, and perhaps inevitably, as so often happens when land and power and money are involved, this was not to be the case.

Broken Promises

Little communication was received from the Bid Team after the announcement in Singapore. The newly formed Olympic Delivery Authority (ODA) then ignored the agreement with TELCO, refused to meet with TELCO's representatives, and even claimed that the Ethical Charter was not their concern, since the ODA had not been in existence when the agreement was signed. Some mild and well-mannered agitation from TELCO followed — including gatherings outside ODA meetings. The

> Land at Olympic Park would be considered for the development of CLT homes only if a "working pilot" could be established.

Authority responded with a letter in 2006 that stated that, whilst the Charter and commitment to a CLT was still an aspiration, the ODA viewed that agreement as nothing more than a memorandum of general understanding "in principle," subject to "considerations of delivery." As such, after the Games, any highly-prized land at the Olympic Park would be considered for the development of CLT homes only if a "working pilot" could be established elsewhere in the city beforehand, as a functioning proof of concept for this unfamiliar model.

What was becoming increasingly clear was that waiting on the Olympic authorities and city officials to deliver London's first CLT was unlikely ever to work, so East London's communities decided to take matters into their own hands. On a bright sunny morning in July 2007, TELCO descended on the land immediately opposite London's City Hall, pitched fifty tents, and refused to move until Mayor Ken Livingstone came out and promised to make some land available for a CLT pilot. After much to-ing and fro-ing — first with his staff and then with the Mayor himself — Livingstone appeared, and pledged that a site would be made available. After snapping some smiling pictures, everyone left, convinced once more that progress towards London's first CLT was being made.

The land that Livingstone eventually proposed, however, was a disused industrial path called Bow Lock on the very eastern edge of the borough of Tower Hamlets: a forgotten space between a main arterial road and the River Lea. The chief problem, however, as TELCO later discovered, was that the land promised by the Mayor was not actually his to gift. Rather than belonging to his office, the land belonged to the local council, which was far less keen on the idea of their land being given away. And so, despite four years of campaigning, come the beginning of 2008, the campaign was back at square one. A new site needed to be found.

The Meeting at Ponti's

It was around this time that the campaign decided it needed to professionalize in terms of its housing expertise, and employ a different organisational structure beyond just the broad-based community organising tactics it had previously utilized. In response to the cry of "Give Us Some Land!," the repost from those in power at the Authority and at City Hall had become clear: "What land? And to Whom? (You expect us to give land to that rabble waving placards?!)."

The East London Citizens Community Land Trust Ltd had been formed in 2007, but up until now it had been just a campaign. Neil Jameson, TELCO's Executive Director, along with Matthew Bolton, the Lead Community Organizer for East London, had long been on the lookout for allies who could help them put a firmer structure in place. Amongst those they discovered was Stephen Hill — a long-established and well-respected housing expert, who after years of working for a number of social housing organisations and public bodies, had taken to doing what he described as "only the interesting and worthwhile work" as a freelance contractor. By chance, he had briefly been employed by the Olympics planners, helping them to run some public workshops around potential uses of the Olympic Park after the Games. It was at one of these meetings — when TELCO had arrived yet again to make a nuisance of themselves — that Stephen quietly mentioned to Neil and Matthew that he was very much "on their side." He offered to meet up afterwards to see if he might help to move things forward.

Around the same time, TELCO appointed its first dedicated Housing Organizer — a twenty-two-year-old named Dave Smith. He had recently returned from a stay in Massachusetts, volunteering on the Obama primary campaign, and was eager to become involved in community organising like that he had read about that was going on in the US. In Neil Jameson's words, he "simply wouldn't leave us alone." This was — by all accounts — Smith's chief, and perhaps only, qualification for being offered the job. Nevertheless, he set about starting to formalize the campaign and to search for a new site. However, given TELCO's limited resources, he could only be paid for one day a week. So the rest of his time was spent keeping bar at a local pub called The Little Driver, at the end of the road where he was living in Bow.

Each Monday, he would walk the mile or so to TELCO's offices in Whitechapel to meet with the formative campaign membership that TELCO had begun to put together, heading along Mile End Road past a disused hospital site called St Clements. His induction to the new job was short — a two-day seminar on Alinsky and organising, and a list of three names of people to meet with. Top of this list was Stephen Hill — who suggested that they meet for coffee at Ponti's Café in the Liverpool Street train station.

THE CAMPAIGN TO ACQUIRE ST CLEMENTS

At that very first meeting, Stephen and Dave discussed the prospect of acquiring the boarded-up St Clement's hospital site as the potential home for London's first CLT. Designed by a renowned architect Richard Tress and constructed in 1849 for £55,000 (a princely sum for that time!), the building had had a succession of occupants and uses over the years. It had originally operated as a workhouse for the poor, with accommodations for 800 inmates. It boasted Siberian marble pillars, a chapel with stained glass, and an elegant Board of Guardians Room for those who oversaw its operations.

As workhouses were phased-out throughout the country, it became the Bow Infirmary in 1874, and was then renamed the Bow Institution in 1912, caring for the long-term sick. The building became a psychiatric unit in 1936 under the new name of St Clement's Hospital. Despite being bombed heavily during the Second World War, it remained a sight to behold, until eventually closing its doors in 2005. Ownership of the land and buildings then reverted from the National Health Service (NHS) to the office of the Mayor of London. The site then sat vacant for years, awaiting its planned sale for private housing development.

Walking along the Mile End Road in 2009, Dave Smith had noticed that the vacant buildings, despite being weathered and derelict, remained architecturally impressive. But from a community organizer's point of view the site was even more special. It straddled almost the exact midpoint of the road running from the center of London to the proposed site for the Olympic Stadium. As he later recalled:

CITY OF LONDON UNION WORKHOUSE.——Mr. R. Tress, Architect.

Fig. 5.2. Original design and purpose of the St Clements site, 1849.

It was in the heart of our power base . . . surrounded by our member institutions. And above all else, it had the capacity to take the campaign out of the abstract — away from theory and policy — and root it in a sense of place for families who needed somewhere to call home. They could actually see themselves potentially living there. And from the moment we first set our sights on it, the campaign truly took off.

The newly revitalized campaign group met for the first time on a cold winter's Saturday in November, in a flat overlooking the muddy expanse that was set to become the Olympic Park. The group had identified four potential sites. A vote on which of these to pursue was taken a few weeks later in a second meeting at Bryant Street Methodist Church. But there was never any question of which site was going to win. Unanimously, the campaign group chose St Clements as its target for developing London's first CLT homes.

Soon after, the campaign took another early giant step forward with the arrival on the scene of Chris Brown, Chief Executive of an ethical property developer named "igloo Regeneration." East London CLT had no track record, little direct development expertise, and only just enough money to pay its one-person staff for one day a week. This fledgling organization needed quickly to transform itself to be able to competitively tender for prime real estate worth tens of millions of pounds in one of the UK's hottest housing markets. The newly elected Board — drawn mostly from the community organising base — met with Chris Brown and entered into a partnership with igloo Regeneration.

Over the next year, this highly progressive developer and the CLT's board collaborated in developing both a competitive housing proposal and a high-profile political campaign to win the tender. As soon as Brown's team were on board, architects were appointed, plans were drawn up, financial modelling was commissioned, and the bid to build London's first CLT homes was at last in full motion. The CLT's founding Chairman, Paul Regan, later said: "Few did more in those early days than Chris Brown — and Stephen Hill throughout — to drag our pipe-dream of acquiring St Clements from a well-meaning longshot to a viable proposition."

> The CLT was given a classic lesson in the trials and tribulations of community-led development.

It was also around this time that a talented young architect named Calum Green — who would go on to lead the organisation in the years ahead — joined the staff team. Pioneering the CLT's community-led design work, he and Dave worked together over the three years that followed, as the tender process was drawn out and the East London CLT was given a classic lesson in the trials and tribulations of community-led development. Reluctant bureaucrats at City Hall sought to temper the public commitments made in front of Citizens Assemblies by Mayor Ken Livingstone and, subsequently, by Mayor Boris Johnson. The tender documents were reissued approximately fifteen times. The multinational private developers who were also bidding for the contract set up a pseudo, one-person "CLT" in order to try and win the competition.

Fig. 5.3. St Clements action, circa 2009.

But the East London CLT persisted, continually building their organisation and their political campaign. The CLT worked closely with local civic institutions in Tower Hamlets, including Darul Ummah and the East London Mosque. Students at Queen Mary, University of London, under the tutelage of Professor Jane Wills, studied the site and assembled data that could be used in planning its redevelopment for lower-income families. And the CLT's Vice-Chair, Colin Glen, and his black-majority New Testament Church of God in Mile End, hosted boisterous Annual General Meetings which kept CLT members and the general public both informed and enthused about the campaign.

Compromise on Everything
Except Your Principles and Winning

The eventual outcome of the tender was a political compromise. It was decided by Mayor Boris Johnson that ownership of the St Clements site should go in part to the East London CLT. This was undoubtedly a win for the organization and set it on the path to becoming the largest CLT in the United Kingdom. But, sadly, he also ruled that the East London CLT/igloo Regeneration bid would not win the contract to redevelop the site. Instead, the City awarded the contract to a private developer, Linden Homes. Because of the political stir the CLT had caused, however, including coverage on the front page of the *London Evening Standard*, the selection of Linden Homes was conditional on the developer being able to strike a deal with the East London CLT to integrate a specified number of resale-restricted CLT homes into the new development.

The pressure from City Hall to build a new relationship and to make it work quickly was now on, but so too was the pressure from the local community to strike a deal that stayed true to the CLT's promises and original purpose. An all-member Open Meeting of the East London CLT was thus called in the Methodist Church opposite the St Clement's site to discuss the forthcoming negotiation with the private developer. The CLT would get 23 homes, slightly fewer than it had sought in its original bid. It would also be forced to abandon the relationship with igloo Regeneration and to team up with a developer with whom the East London CLT had no prior relationship in order to deliver a scheme that differed drastically from the CLT's community-led designs. On the other hand, the option on the table was still significant. Andy Schofield, a founding Board Member and later the CLT's Project Director, led the Open Meeting. A hundred people participated in a formal discussion of what they felt "a CLT must be," "a CLT could be," and "a CLT could not be."

Inspired by their community organising training — which draws upon the lessons of Thucydides and the debate between the Athenians and the islanders of Melos — East London CLT members collectively crafted a negotiating position that reflected their priorities:

* The CLT must deliver permanent affordability;

- The St Clement's project should be based-upon principles of community-led design, so the site plans proposed by the developer should be revisited and redrawn; and

- The CLT's homes must not be controlled, managed, or owned by other parties.

With the battle lines drawn, the Board Chair and the Director for the East London CLT headed into their first meeting with executives from Linden Homes in a hotel just opposite Buckingham Palace. The CLT's representatives had a magnificent platform from which to press their case, due to the power of ordinary citizens organizing. Three hours later, with all of the CLT's conditions met, the deal for London's first community land trust project was signed. It was April 2012.

THREE LESSONS FOR CLTs EVERYWHERE

The story goes on from there — through a series of community-led design charrettes and a total redesign of the site plan; through the planning application process; through the financial and contractual negotiations; to the ground-breaking in March 2014, which featured Mayor Boris Johnson happily driving a bulldozer around the site. There were ups and downs along the way, too numerous to tell. But for those of us who went through the whole process — many of whom are still actively involved today, in what has since expanded and so been renamed the London CLT — there have been three lessons within our experience that we believe to be relevant to the CLT movement worldwide.

1. A "Classically" English CLT?

The first is a reflection upon an incredibly important debate: namely, to what extent should the "classic" CLT model — with its history, its proven track record, but also its chiefly American practice and legal construct — be open to interpretation and change in other countries? And how should a new organisation find the appropriate balance between adapting the model to meet local conditions, whilst maintaining a common understanding of the model's features and purpose, among all organisations that wish to call themselves a CLT?

Definitions and explanations of the CLT model in the UK are inherently ambiguous, and intentionally so. When the community land trust was first written into law as part of the Housing and Regeneration Act of 2008, the CLT pioneers who drafted that legislation did so in a manner they believed would allow CLTs to be expansive and innovative. Their proposal was adopted with minimal alteration. As a result, there were no statutory requirements for a CLT to follow the "classic" model, as it had evolved in the United States, nor was there any mention in the law of the necessity of ensuring the permanent affordability. The law said only that a CLT was *"to ensure that the assets are not sold or developed except in a manner which the trust's members think benefits the local community."*

A case could be made that such organizational ambiguity, where a CLT may be organized and operated in many ways, has been essential to the growth and success of CLTs in the UK. The London CLT chose very consciously, however, to adopt many of the traits of the "classic" model. Outward looking, it drew a clear line of distinction between CLTs and established housing associations and co-ops in the UK, which had long provided affordable housing of various types, but which didn't involve the community in the same way.

The result was an organization that is structured as closely to the "classic" CLT as possible within the legal confines of the UK system. In fact, the London CLT follows the American tradition more closely than any other CLT currently established in the UK. This was not without its problems. In many ways, there are tasks that would probably have been more quickly and readily achieved had the organization entirely anglicized its structures. But the organizers, leaders, and members of the London CLT felt that a too drastic departure from the "classic" model would excessively distance themselves from a growing international CLT movement. They felt strongly aligned to that movement, so they wanted to promote a structure and purpose that were consistent with most other CLTs in the world.

The resulting arrangements, at least on paper, can look somewhat messy. The tripartite composition of the London CLT's board does not always resonate immediately with members and needs constant explaining. And leaseholder laws in the UK mean that "owning the land" outright is both far less common and less simple than elsewhere. (London CLT does not own the "freehold" at St Clements in the same way as CLTs elsewhere, but in terms of local property laws this is a technicality rather than a meaningful distinction.)

Fig. 5.4. Board of directors, London Community Land Trust, 2019.

As such, we have come to conclude, much like John Davis said on one of several visits to the London CLT, that CLT organizers must confront the difficult challenge of finding the right balance between adopting the "classic" model and adapting that model to their own peculiar local and national circumstances, for the sake of balancing practical challenges and maintaining a movement worldwide. Davis went on to say:

> It was absolutely essential for us [in the United States] to develop a common language, a common understanding of what a CLT is. Without that, it was hard to distinguish the CLT from competing models, competing traditions; it was hard to draw people together under the banner of CLTs until there was a common vocabulary. Conversely, once you have agreement as to what a CLT is, it gives you the freedom to innovate within that structure and to improve the "classic" model . . . . But if you modify too much, you risk severing the connection to our roots, to our values, to the sense of purpose and struggle that comes from them. . . . So a common understanding of the model creates a yardstick of values and performance against which you can assess whether a proposed innovation will help or hinder.

2. Linking House Prices to Local Wages to Create True Affordability

The second lesson we learned is the importance of a locally-determined definition of the term "affordable housing." In the UK, following changes made by the national government in 2010, the term "affordable housing" became a source of derision, having been adjudicated in law to mean anything "up to 80% of the open-market rate," which in London is now rarely affordable to anyone. As such, the term has lost all meaning. Yet, in the first instance, the London CLT had planned to devise its sales values in a similar way. The original plan had been to sell fixed, capped-equity shares at approximately 60% of the open-market value. That changed in October 2011, when board members and staff from the London CLT attended the National CLT Conference in the United States.

As part of that conference, after a long boat journey from Seattle to OPAL Community Land Trust in the San Juan Islands, the visitors from London had an in-depth conversation with Lisa Byers, OPAL's Executive Director. Thoughtful and eloquent in her exposition, she extolled the virtues of linking the cost of homes not to any percentage of the open market value — "which we all accept is an inherently broken and an unrelated assessment of what people on local wages can afford"— and tying it instead to a multiplier of average local incomes. This was a transformative moment for the London CLT, for it not only provided a clear mechanism for its stated aim of delivering "truly affordable homes," but also provided the CLT with a unique and compelling narrative for what it was about —"homes that local people on local wages can afford."

Back home, those on the trip crunched the numbers and — after a lot of work with local groups to gut-check the impact of this new resale formula — established their own wholly unique but quite brilliant mechanism by which the homes were to be sold. Prices were to be determined by: (a) taking the median average wage in the area in which the homes were to be built; (b) applying the principle that no family should be forced to spend more than one third of their income on housing; and then (c) multiplying this figure out by a standard set of mortgage assumptions (e.g., 25-years at an average rate of interest and with a 10% downpayment). This calculation yielded a price that local people could genuinely afford to pay — a price that was created by working backward from their own circumstances, rather than being derived from market conditions. If residents ever chose to move, they would be bound to apply the same formula in calculating the resale price of their homes. CLT house prices would always rise in line with wage inflation, therefore, rather than rising in relation to market-driven house and land prices that are increasingly beholden to the whim of foreign investors or buy-to-leave landlords.

> London CLT strives to be not only a social justice campaign, but also the best consumer choice.

The London CLT — which strives to be not only a social justice campaign, but also the best consumer choice available to any median-income household — had found its niche. With three-bedroom houses (including a garden) at St Clements going on sale for £235,000 ($295,000) through the CLT, compared to costs starting at £600,000 ($755,000) for market-rate homes offered next door by the private developer, the London CLT had created a defining, replicable, and sustainable proposition for permanently affordable housing across the city.

3. Keeping Community in the CLT

The third and most important reflection on this journey is that, above all else, community land trusts must "keep the C in CLT." It is this, ultimately, that lies at the heart of the St Clement's story. Community is what gives the London CLT its greatest potential for having lasting success, whilst at the same helping the CLT to stay rooted to its original purpose and promise. In the UK — where the provision of affordable housing has long been established through state-run council housing — it is the CLT's *relational* rather than *bureaucratic* culture, its focus on people as individuals rather than as numbers, that sets it apart.

One of the clearest examples of this relational aspect in the St Clement's process came when one of our first residents (a family who had been with the campaign throughout and had passed through the CLT's allocations process and affordability assessment) was refused a mortgage at the last minute by their lender. This was due to a technicality, based on previous debts which were not wholly theirs. In such circumstances, the easiest thing to do from a risk management perspective, and what most other traditional affordable housing providers would have done, would have been to rescind the offer and to go to the next family on the waiting list. But the governing board of the London CLT took a conscious decision not to do this. Instead, the board spent a lot of time and political capital

Fig. 5.5. London CLT Annual General Meeting, 10-year anniversary, September 2017.

negotiating with the local housing authority so as to achieve a planning amendment, which allowed the family to rent the property until they could qualify for a mortgage. That way, they could move into their new home and wouldn't have their hopes dashed yet again. The London CLT stands by our people — our mission starts and ends with them rather than rigidly following any bureaucratic or abstract quasi-utilitarian definition of "housing need."

But this family's story also illustrates a further obstacle that the London CLT has had to overcome. One of the hallmarks of doing housing development in the UK (and in much of Europe as well) is that it takes a very long time to plan, design, finance, and complete every project. This poses an enormous challenge for CLT practitioners: How do you keep prospective homebuyers interested? How do you keep the larger community of members and allies actively engaged throughout? How do you keep your power from bleeding away while waiting for something to get built?

In this regard, we would contend that building the organisation is as important as building the homes themselves. London CLT has always put a strong emphasis on its non-housing activities as a way of ensuring that our wider social justice mission is supported and sustained. One of the best examples of this — when trying in the early days to get the local community involved with the redesign of St Clements — was the work of then board members Kate MacTiernan and Lizzy Daish who, in collaboration with film director and East End resident, Danny Boyle, put on the Shuffle Film Festival for the CLT. Held over the course of a week, it opened up the St Clements site to the local community and helped them to re-engage with it, to reimagine what had been a rather sad place, and to reconceive of it as a new, accessible and exciting opportunity.

THE END OF THE BEGINNING

The London CLT at St Clements has never been just about delivering permanently affordable homes. More than that, it is about community, social justice and, quite simply, contributing to happiness in life and emotional well-being.

When our very first residents, Humayra and Ruman and their young baby Yunus, whose parents had immigrated to the East End from Bangladesh in late 1960s, moved into their new CLT home, you could see how much it meant to their whole family. In Ruman's own words:

> Before we moved into St Clement's, we were living with my parents, brother, and sister. There were six of us all in one flat. My wife (Humayra) and I shared a room whilst we had a baby on the way. It was not easy to live as a family within a family — it meant my wife felt like a stranger in her own home. I remember the day we moved in well — my whole extended family turned up. It was pouring with rain but I was beaming inside. There is so much space! I feel really lucky we get to own our own home — it has changed my family's life. There was a moment the other day when Humayra, Yunus and I were in the flat, and my Dad came over. He sat on the sofa with his arms spread out and he burst out into singing some sort of oldy goldy traditional Bengali song. My Dad only sings when he is feeling the happiest he's felt in years. That's how you know when Dad's happy; he doesn't smile, he sings. When you have that sense of space, it opens up your mind. He felt that, and he had to let it out.

Since then, Humayra has given birth to a little girl, making her the first baby born in a London CLT home! There will, we hope, be many more to come. Because the CLT movement, above all else, starts and ends with people and their lives — not housing, or resale formulas, or anything else.

To that end, many more people should be mentioned and thanked. And whilst to write an exhaustive list is impossible, and the injustice of omission is great, it would be wrong not to mention at least the incredible work along the way of Pablo Absalud, Sister Una McCreish, Fr. Sean Connolly, Fr. Tom O'Brien, David Rodgers, Peter Ambrose, Suzanne Gormann, Miranda Housden, Professor Tim Oliver, Fr. Angus Ritchie, Bethan Lant, Ruhana Ali, Nick Durie, Colin Ivermee, Tim Carey, Joe Ball, Jenny Lumley, Neil Hunt, Lina Jamoul, Emmanuel Gatora, Sebastien Chapleau, Alison Gelder, Ruby Mahera, Nano McCaughan, Hannah Emery-Wright, Ben Cole, Grace Boyle, Charles Campion, the Butler Family Fund, and the Oak Foundation. This is as much their story as it is the story of our residents and of the homes we have built.

Whilst the first 23 homes at St Clements may not be everything we set out to achieve, and whilst they most definitely have not solved the housing crisis in our city, they have proved one thing beyond doubt: when local communities get together and organize, and when the universal principles of the CLT are carefully applied, it does not matter what city you are in, or how challenging the market may be, because what we do works. There is no mission impossible.

Fig. 5.6. Future residents of St Clements, looking out the window of their home-to-be, January 2018.

6.

From Pressure Group to Government Partner

The Story of the Brussels Community Land Trust

Geert De Pauw and Nele Aernouts

A housing crisis has been raging in the Brussels Capital Region for decades. The failure of government to address this problem prompted neighborhood associations and housing rights activists in Brussels to join forces in 2008 and to look for solutions of their own. In their search, they stumbled upon an Anglo-Saxon model that had remained largely unnoticed in the European mainland: the community land trust. It seemed to comprise everything they were looking for.

In 2013, the Community Land Trust Brussels (CLTB) was established and received support from the regional government. The first newly constructed CLT homes were inhabited in 2015, and new housing projects are now being built at various locations in Brussels. Meanwhile, CLTB has been playing an important role in disseminating the CLT model in Europe.

In this chapter, we will provide an overview of the housing crisis in Brussels. We will then discuss the origins of the Brussels CLT. Starting the CLT was relatively quick and easy, but the road to putting the organization on a firm footing has not been without challenges. From the beginning, CLTB has had to cope with a number of legal, organisational, and institutional barriers. We will discuss some of these struggles and the agreements put in place to resolve them, before concluding with a look at future prospects for CLT growth in Brussels.

I. WELCOME TO BRUSSELS, CAPITAL OF EUROPE!

The implementation of a CLT in the Brussels Capital Region can only be understood within the context of the region's chronic housing problems. For several decades, a substantial fraction of the housing stock has been unaffordable for a considerable share of the population. A severe mismatch between average household incomes and average housing prices is at the core of the problem: for half of households living in Brussels, the share of their household budget going to pay for housing exceeds 40% (Romainville, 2009). This problem, which academics and housing activists have come to term a "housing crisis," is based on several dichotomies and inadequate policy responses.

A Socio-Economic Dichotomy

Since the restructuring of the labor market in the 1980s, the Brussels Capital Region has been marked by considerable economic growth. This growth has been driven by the service sector, which is dominated by European, federal, and regional administrations and has attracted international and multi-national corporations (Loopmans & Kesteloot, 2009).

This economic growth is not entirely to the benefit of the population residing within Brussels, nor are the benefits of growth shared evenly among them. Here are a few indications. Half of the jobs in the Brussels Capital Region (BCR) are held by inhabitants of Belgium's two other regions, Wallonia and Flanders, who commute into Brussels on a daily basis. Among all of the regions in Europe, the BCR is ranked 4th in Gross Domestic Product (GDP),[1] but it is ranked 145th when it comes to the disposable household income of BCR's population (Englert et al., 2018). The BCR also exhibits a pattern of high levels of poverty and large numbers of people on welfare. The percentage of BCR's population who are at risk of poverty is significantly higher than in Belgium's other regions: 39% of the Brussels population is at risk of poverty, compared to 27% in Wallonia and 14% in Flanders.[2] At least 23% of the children in Brussels are growing up in households in which no income is earned through the job market (Englert et al., 2018).

An External and Internal Migration Dichotomy

Another dichotomy can be identified when looking at external and internal migration patterns, fueled by different streams of migration following World War II. Among all inhabitants of the Brussels Capital Region, 35% of them have a non-Belgian nationality, while 72% have non-Belgian origins.[3] On the one side of the spectrum, every expansion of the EU brings highly skilled EU migrants and an increased attractiveness for foreign corporations and new highly skilled migrants (Englert et al., 2018). On the other side, the migration waves of the 1960s and 1970s brought mainly Moroccan and Italian guest workers, few of whom were able to climb the social ladder due to the economic crises of the mid-1970s and 1980s. Later on, these immigrants were joined by family members and a more diverse group of new immigrants. They have often ended up in informal or low-paid economic circuits, such as the building, cleaning, transport and catering sectors (Loopmans & Kesteloot, 2008).

Spatially, the high-skilled native and foreign populations have settled in peripheral municipalities, while lower-income groups have found housing in the more central, post-industrial neighborhoods of Brussels along the Canal, an area known as the "poor crescent" (Kesteloot, 2000).[4] For decades, this area has been dealing with severe problems of housing quality that range from moisture problems to a lack of heating systems, and to phenomena such as overcrowding and subletting (Englert et al., 2018). In more recent years, problems of affordability have also emerged.

Inadequate Policy Responses

Public policy has historically given an inadequate answer to these dichotomies. From its very inception, Belgian housing policy has been marked by an anti-urban attitude, represented by a persistent priority for stimulating homeownership outside of the cities. Spatial planning policies, meanwhile, have been nearly absent (Dedecker, 2008).

Belgian housing policy has had its greatest impact on the residential movements of upwardly mobile families, supporting homeownership outside of cities through fiscal grants and cheap railway tickets. From the 1950s onward, families in search of a green, less-dense environment were helped to buy houses in the peripheries outside the Brussels Capital Region. This focus on homeownership didn't change fundamentally after the regionalization of the nation's housing policy.[5] Today, half of the region's housing budget goes to supporting homeownership, a policy intended to keep middle-class households within the BCR and, simultaneously, to increase tax revenues. This public support for homeownership takes the form of tax deductions,[6] soft mortgages,[7] and direct grants for the development of housing serving homeowners with modest incomes.[8] Such development has often been concentrated in the "poor crescent," in order to increase the area's "social mix" and to create a domino effect of attracting further private investment.[9]

> The amount of social housing is stuck at 7.5%, even though half of the population qualifies for social housing.

Despite taking such a large share of the housing policy budget, the homeownership rate has declined during the last decades, due primarily to a steep rise in housing prices.[10] Furthermore, among the beneficiaries of this homeownership policy, middle-income households are overrepresented. These households enjoy the benefit of this "extra encouragement," but are not necessarily in need of additional funding to become homeowners (Dessouroux et al., 2016, p.24).

The persistent focus on conventional, market-priced homeownership has impeded the growth of community-based housing and creation of a decent social rental market (Geurts and Goossens, 2004). Today, the amount of social housing is stuck at 7.5%, even though half of the BCR's population qualifies for social housing (Englert et al., 2018). Due to the small amount of social housing, there is excessive demand in the private rental market, which allows landlords to impose strict requirements for the selection of tenants. Not surprisingly, these requirements are characterized by discrimination and racism, especially targeting prospective tenants with a social assistance benefit or a disability benefit and/or those having a particular ethnic background (Heylen & Van den Broeck, 2015).

The BCR launched several programs to build additional social housing, but very few homes have been constructed and the impact on the housing crisis has been close to zero.

Urban policies and programs aimed at the redevelopment of inner-city neighborhoods have been inadequate at best and harmful at worst, with regard to affordable housing. (Dessouroux et al., 2016). For decades after putting into effect the 1953 slum-clearing law (*Wet op de Krotopruiming*) and high-rise replacements of the 1960s and 1970s, no decent urban renewal program was developed to address the deterioration of under-privileged areas. Deindustrialization in the Belgian economy left these neighborhoods with a deteriorating housing stock, poor-quality public spaces and an impoverished, transient and aging population. Not until 1993, with the introduction of "neighbor-hood contracts" by the Brussels government, did public policy begin to tackle these problems. These "contracts" enhanced local regeneration through investment in pub-lic spaces and services, programs to promote social-economic integration, renovations of buildings, and the construction of housing on residual parcels (Vermeulen, 2009).

Two additional policies for territorial development, the Regional Zoning Plan (2012) and the International Development Plan (2018), focused on revitalization of the area and the development of housing along the Canal.

The urban policies of the past twenty-five years have been widely praised for tak-ing a more integrated and inclusionary approach to neighborhood development and for explicitly addressing the social-spatial fragmentation of Brussels. But there has also been a darker, less praiseworthy side to these policies. The reservation of large lands for redevelopment by private investors and the repeated mantra in government policies and plans of needing a better "social mix" in inner-city neighborhoods have had an implicit aim: attracting higher-income groups to these areas. As public and private investment increases, however, land values and housing prices rise, making it harder for lower-in-come people to gain access to affordable housing.

In sum, the benefits of economic growth in the Brussels Capital Region have been inequitably shared across geographic areas and across social classes. Patterns of gentrifica-tion have been supported by a housing and urban policy promoting the revitalization of inner-city neighborhoods. These economic and social realities, combined with a housing system fraught with problems of deterioration, discrimination, unaffordability, and the meagre production of social housing, eventually pushed concerned activists and com-munity organizations into the housing domain, seeking alternatives to forms of housing provided by either the state or the market.

II. CREATION OF THE BRUSSELS COMMUNITY LAND TRUST

In 2007, the "Ministry of Housing Crisis," a grassroots initiative launched by squatters, homeless people, community organizations, and housing activists, occupied the empty Gesu Monastery in Sint Joost to call attention to the housing problem. In addition to initiatives asking the government to take responsibility for the housing crisis, there were also experiments with new solutions. For instance, the community center, Bonnevie, initiated l'Espoir in the municipality of Molenbeek with the support of CIRE, an association that mainly works with refugees and newcomers. CIRE had previously developed solidarity savings groups, where low-income families collectively save money to finance the purchase of individual homes. The l'Espoir housing project produced fourteen affordable, energy-efficient, owner-occupied homes. The low-income families who purchased these homes were closely involved in the project's development, right from the start. Through design workshops, they influenced the building plans, they started a savings group to prepare for the purchase of the homes, and they became an important partner in discussions during the building process, alongside Fonds du Logement (the developer), the architect, and the municipality (De Pauw, 2011).

The l'Espoir housing project successfully linked a dimension of collective endeavor and solidarity to individual homeownership. However, the sponsors realized that the classic homeownership formula used in this project did not provide a structural solution for the housing crisis. The project required substantial subsidies from government to make it work, which would be lost whenever the homes were subsequently resold. Nor were there guarantees against future speculation. The project's sponsors started looking for an alternative strategy that would make the homes permanently affordable and would structurally integrate resident participation into the design and operation of the housing.

In the United States they discovered the CLT model, which was largely unknown on the European mainland until then. In September 2009, the British Building and Social Housing Foundation (named World Habitat today) invited four community developers from Brussels to take part in an international study visit to the Champlain Housing Trust in Burlington, Vermont.[11] After a week, the group returned to Brussels convinced that the CLT model was what they were looking for. During a conference on cooperative housing in Brussels, they publicly launched the plan to start campaigning for the creation of a CLT in Brussels, which was received with great interest.

This eventually led to a charter for the establishment of the Community Land Trust Brussels. The charter was signed on May 25, 2010 by fifteen associations. During three public meetings, the concept was explained and discussed with the participants: families in need of housing, community organizers, housing rights activists, and academics interested in the model. Hundreds of people participated in these events, while a small core group met regularly to set out a strategy and to seek further support for the plan. Out of this dynamic, the Platform Community Land Trust Brussels, the precursor of the Brussels CLT, eventually grew.[12] The Platform, a group of supportive organisations, set itself the aim of promoting the CLT model in Brussels. The organization's leaders wrote a few articles about their ideas, talked to the press, and arranged a series of trainings, lectures, film performances, and public assemblies to explain the model. They started to develop scenarios for the establishment of a CLT in Brussels and to search for subsidies to make this happen. In 2011, the Green Minister for Housing of the Brussels Capital Region commissioned a feasibility study. The recommendations of the study were put into practice in 2012 and led to establishment of the actual community land trust.

In Brussels, the CLT is composed of two bodies, a nonprofit association and a Foundation. Both were officially founded in 2012. The Region granted a subsidy covering the costs of development for CLTB's first housing project. Financial support from the Brussels Capital Region enabled CLTB to start constructing dwellings that could be made affordable for the lowest income groups soon after its formation. Monies from the government also financed the creation of a team of four people who started working for CLTB in September 2012.

In 2013, community land trusts were included in the Brussels' Housing Code.[13] The Code mentioned CLTs alongside existing tools such as social rental housing and social mortgages. It defined what CLTs are and stated that the government could define, in an implementing law, the rules according to which CLTs could get recognized by the Region. To date, this law hasn't been drafted, but the fact that CLTs were quoted in the Code had an important symbolical function.

In 2014, the government secured the financing of CLT operations by including CLTB as a participant in the Housing Alliance. This investment program for new affordable housing in the Brussels region ensured that 2 million euros could be invested each year between 2014 and 2018 for the development of new CLT projects. CLTB could use this money for the acquisition of land and for covering a part of the construction costs.

Early Projects

Together with local partner associations, CLTB has created a development pipeline of twelve projects to date. Most of them are located in neighborhoods of the "poor crescent," adding to an "in situ" regeneration of these areas. These projects include a total of more than 180 dwellings and six spaces for community infrastructure. Almost all of the projects are multi-family homes. The first CLTB project, *l'Ecluse* (9 homes), has been inhabited since 2015. Five new projects are in construction; five others are being prepared.

The *Arc-en-Ciel* project in Molenbeek, the largest project until now, is one of CLTB's flagships. The vacant land that used to include a house and workshop was bought in 2013. However, due to several delays within the construction process, notably for obtaining the building permit, it took more than six years to build *Arc-en-Ciel*. Together with the Housing Fund,[14] a social housing agency, and several partner associations, CLTB developed 32 dwellings, a community garden, and a women's community center on this land. Since the very beginning, the future residents have been intensively involved in the project's development, participating in architecture workshops, assemblies, and general meetings. Construction was completed at the end of 2019 and the homeowners began moving into their new homes.

Fig 6.1. l'Ecluse, CLTB's first homes. MARC DETIFFE

A kilometer away, in the municipality of Anderlecht, an old Parish Centre is being transformed into seven owner-occupied homes, a community garden, and a building for a neighborhood association. This project was also launched in 2013. The group of future residents was composed that same year. They called their project *Le Nid*, which means "the Nest." Like *Arc-en-Ciel*, construction was completed in the summer of 2019.

The *Liedts* project, which includes four senior dwellings above a service center in Schaerbeek, focuses on intergenerational living.

The most emblematic project in preparation is called CALICO. This project, constructed by a private developer, is funded by the European Union through an Urban Innovative Actions grant.[15] To obtain this funding, CLTB partnered with two cohousing groups. One of them focuses on women and gender issues, while the other aims to develop a "home for birth and end-of-life" where women can give birth and the elderly can spend their last days in a warm, homelike environment. The project consists of 34 dwellings, the home for birth and end-of-life, and a community center. It focuses on solidarity and community care and is scheduled for completion in 2021.

Finally, one single-family home deserves special mention. In a city as dense and expensive as Brussels, CLTB didn't consider single-family dwellings a possibility. It took two devoted families to convince CLTB of the contrary. An elderly couple who lived near the *l'Ecluse* CLT project was looking for a smaller, single-story dwelling that might better fit their age and family size. Their house with a garden had become too big for them to handle after their children left home. They met one of the families living in *l'Ecluse*, who was looking for a bigger home after their family had expanded. The families decided to swap homes. Doing so, the first family offered the land under the house to CLTB, in order to make it affordable for the family from *l'Ecluse* and to preserve its affordability for generations to come. CLTB hopes this example can inspire others, thus creating affordable homes without any subsidies.

III. CREATIVITY AND REFLEXIVITY

In the beginning, the idea to develop a CLT in the Brussels Capital Region was met with a lot of skepticism from housing experts and politicians. It was said that such a "North American model" could not be applied in Europe. The legal systems were too different; the gap between common law and civil law too great. Other criticisms were aimed at the residents of CLT housing. The community-led process inherent in the CLT model was said to be intertwined with an Anglo-Saxon tradition that was foreign to Belgium. The low-income groups inhabiting CLT projects would not properly take care of their homes, leading to a decrease in property values. The collectively led model would need too much public funding.

Although the Brussels CLT was established relatively quickly, the initiators had to face all of these criticisms and challenges. They were forced to apply a strong dose of creativity and reflexivity throughout their praxis in developing strategies to cope with them, beginning with the problem of legally separating ownership of the dwellings from ownership of the land.

A Bundle of Property Rights

Similar to CLTs in other countries, CLTB includes resale conditions in its land lease contracts in order to keep its homes permanently affordable. This is a renewable, fifty-year right in which CLTB gives the residents permission to own a dwelling on land that is not theirs. An owner may resell his/her property whenever he or she wants, but the resale price is limited and the CLTB will indicate to whom the property must be sold. In this way, the dwellings remain affordable without the government having to invest a second time. Owners are also not allowed to rent out their dwellings, except under certain conditions and for a social rent specified in the land lease. Otherwise, CLTB homeowners have the same rights and obligations as any other homeowner.

CLTB largely modelled its own land lease contracts, resale formulas, bylaws and regulations on those of CLTs in the United States. Integrating the North American community land trust model into the Belgian legal system was not a simple matter, however. Especially challenging was to find a legal solution to separating the ownership of land and dwellings, but this proved to be easier for CLT organizers to accomplish in Belgium than for CLT organizers in the United Kingdom, another common law country.

Belgian law includes two rights that enable the separation of land from the buildings on it: the surface right (*droit de superficie*) and the long-term lease (*bail emphytéotique*). The biggest difference between these two rights is the maximum duration, 50 years for the first and 99 years for the second. Neither can be automatically renewed and extended beyond the maximum period, presenting a potential obstacle to a CLT's commitment to preserve the permanent affordability of land and housing. That is one of the reasons these rights haven't been commonly used for housing.

There is a significant exception, though. In the early 1970s, a new university town was built in Belgium, inspired by contemporary innovations in urban planning. The city of Louvain-la-Neuve was constructed entirely on a concrete slab, separating underground car traffic and parking from overground pedestrian traffic. The land on which the university town is built is owned by the university, which leases out parcels under the principle of *bail emphytéotique*. The houses on these leaseholds are mainly owned by residents or private landlords. The leasehold contracts contain a clause that ensures that, each time a house changes hands, a new duration of 99 years begins to run. By "re-starting the clock" for each new homeowner, a leasehold comes very close to being permanent.

In Louvain-la-Neuve, however, no anti-speculative conditions were attached to the land leases.[16] The university remains the owner of the land, but it does not have the right to restrict price increases on resale of the dwellings. It is doubtful the university wanted to do so, but it is also true that it is difficult to regulate resale prices under *bail emphytéotique* due to the strong protection of property rights within Belgian law. Even if a buyer and seller were to agree to accept a number of contractual resale conditions, there would always be the risk of a court overturning them, deciding such restrictions to be in conflict with property rights.

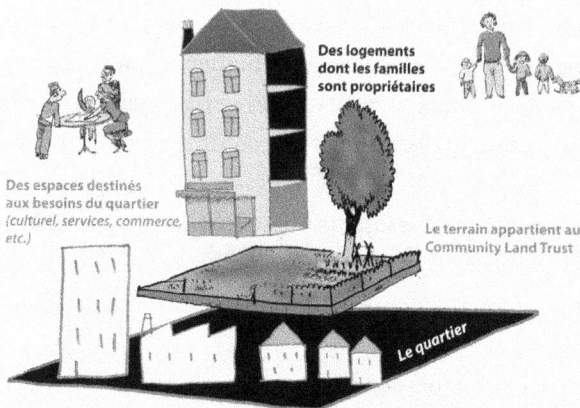

Fig 6.2. Detail of poster created by the Brussels CLT, illustrating the separate ownership of land and buildings.

It is easier to impose restrictions on the resale price, as well as other conditions concerning the use of the home, through the shorter 50-year duration of the *droit de superficie*. Therefore CLTB finally opted for the *droit de superficie*, combining clauses similar to those used in Louvain-la-Neuve with clauses, such as restricting the resale price, thereby creating a lease that is close to everlasting. This leads to fairly complex contracts. Since almost all CLTB dwellings are part of condominiums, even more conditions and variations get added to the ground lease depending on the building developer and on whether the building is renovated or newly constructed.

Undoubtedly, the government could play an important role in the future by facilitating the development of specific legislation oriented towards this variety of property regimes, specifying conditions on the use of the dwelling, the condominium, and the land on which the project is built. Such legislation could simplify the contracts and enhance the legal enforceability of the conditions.

Supporting and Strengthening the CLT Community

CLTB is composed of two closely affiliated legal entities: a nonprofit association[17] responsible for the day-to-day operations; and a public utility foundation[18] that owns the land. They are connected to each other through their bylaws. Both are run by a board of directors whose members include three groups of stakeholders: residents living in dwellings on CLTB land or waiting for a CLT home; representatives of civil society, including members of partner organizations and neighbors of CLT homes; and representatives of the Brussels government. Each stakeholder group gets one-third of the seats.[19]

In contrast to the practice of most CLTs in the United States, once people are interested in buying a house from the CLT, they must become a member of CLTB. As a member of the association, they are automatically registered on a waiting list, and are entitled to vote in electing their representatives to the managing board. Each year some hundred members gather in the general assembly to elect their representatives. These meetings are always one of the highlights of CLTB's community life.

In order to purchase a property from CLTB, households must meet the same income qualifications as required for renting in social housing. While this is a maximum income limit, CLTB is also committed to serving people whose income is even lower. To make this possible, it sets different selling prices depending on the income of the buyers. To this end, the target group is divided into four different income categories. Depending on the income category in which a homebuyer falls, he or she will pay a higher or lower price for the same type of dwelling. Homes for each of these four categories will be realized in each new project. Members on top of the waiting list get priority, according to their income category and their family size.

When launching a new housing project, future residents are selected from the waiting list and brought together in a "project group."[20] These future residents are involved in the design and preparation of the housing project and will be in charge of its management, once the dwellings are built and occupied.

It is stating the obvious that the participation of such a mixed community in the collective management of both CLTB and its projects, a community that includes professionals from ministerial cabinets, social workers, and low-income groups, can be complicated.

Fig 6.3. Project group for a future CLTB project, Luminiere du Nord.

But CLTB is convinced such a mix of interests and perspectives is essential. Through the participation of public officials and civil society, CLTB tries to ensure a long-term integration of public concerns and common interests, such as the integration of the dwelling within the neighborhood, the importance of affordable housing for low-income groups, and the necessity of developing a certain amount of dwellings. Similarly, the active participation of future residents, even when many of them are low-skilled and some have only a basic level of French,[21] is deemed by CLTB to be indispensable, since all decisions that are made will concern their future well-being. Once installed in their homes, they become responsible for keeping the condominium going. As condominium owners, they will have to ensure that the common charges are paid, that costs are correctly distributed, that necessary repairs are made, that a reserve fund is created, and so on. Training and guidance are key, therefore, to preparing and supporting residents in the management of their own housing.

The preparation period, which can sometimes take more than five years, is used to train residents about their legal rights and obligations; the architecture, use, and maintenance of their dwelling; and the management of a multi-unit project. To do this, CLTB collaborates with local partner organizations, who organize training sessions and individually supervise the members of the group. This leads to the establishment of important agreements and initiatives. Future residents draw up a set of rules and divide the dwellings in joint consultation; they write a charter on how they want to live together; and they take

Fig. 6.4. Annual General Meeting, Brussels CLT, 2015.

the initiative in introducing the project to people who already live in the neighborhood.

In Molenbeek, for instance, every month the *Arc-en-Ciel* group organizes the Bazar Festival on the pavement in front of the construction site of their housing project. The Bazar Festival is a festive flea market for the neighborhood. Members of the project groups have indicated how all of this helps them to acquire new skills, to cultivate self-confidence, and to strengthen the cohesion in the group (Aernouts & Ryckewaert, 2017).

Another strategy to strengthen the (future) residents and to help them in taking up their role in these different levels of management is to actively bring together the somewhat artificial CLTB community. This community is made up of approximately two hundred sympathizers and nearly four hundred families who would like someday to obtain a home through CLTB. They live in different places in the Brussels Region and usually do not know each other when they sign on as a member. They meet each other, at best, only at the annual general meeting. CLTB has now started a membership program that wants to overcome this separation and unfamiliarity among this large constituency. The program aims to strengthen both the connections among individual members and solidarity across the entire community by developing collective projects outside of the housing domain. Thanks to this program, CLTB's members have set up a group that organizes cycling lessons, they have organized the temporary use of buildings that are awaiting demolition or renovation, and they have participated in fundraising activities for CLTB.

Institutionalisation without Bureaucratization?

CLTB has grown from an informal citizens' initiative into a professional organization in just a few years. The number of dwellings produced is still limited, mainly due to the long duration of the development of real estate projects in Brussels. The plan, from now on, is to deliver twenty to thirty new homes annually. But CLTB has the ambition to increase production even further, with a goal of having a thousand dwellings on its land by 2030.

Whether this is possible will largely depend on political support and the willingness of governmental bodies to continue making funds and lands available. The growth of the organization's portfolio and CLTB's strong dependence on governmental resources for such growth pose a number of challenges.

First, as a consequence of this dependence, CLTB is obliged to follow strict policies and procedures required by governmental entities for certain aspects of CLTB's daily operation. Aspirations and value systems of CLTB and public institutions are not always similar, and strict governmental frameworks have an impact on CLTB's autonomy. For instance, when using public subsidies, CLTB is obliged to adopt public tendering procedures, complicating the participative nature of the development process.

Second, CLTB is particularly vulnerable to political changes (Aernouts, 2017); that is, every change in the regional government can lead to a new positioning of acceptance and support for the community land trust model. Every four years, CLTB has to win the trust of the political party in charge and enter into a new relationship. Strategic battles and power games between political parties add to the difficulty. In the beginning of 2017, for instance, a regime change within the regional government led to the party in power giving serious consideration to forcing the CLT Brussels to transfer ownership of its lands to other housing providers in Brussels. Fortunately, thanks to the efforts of a strong network of supporters, this proposal, which would have undermined the entire rationale and operation of CLTB, was not adopted. But it demonstrates CLTB's vulnerability to changes in the political wind.

Meanwhile, political support for the CLT model is growing. After the regional elections in May 2019, the new government, composed of social democrats, greens, and regionalists, presented its coalition agreement. It stated that all public housing operators should make greater use of long-term lease contracts and that the government should "increase its support for the projects developed by Community Land Trust Brussels" and recognize CLTB as a "regional land alliance," accompanied by a management agreement so that CLTB can become "a partner in urban renewal programs."

Thirdly, the increase in scale and professionalization adds a dose of bureaucratization to CLTB's operations, even as the organization strives to remain a community-led movement that is guided and governed by its members. Also, as the number of inhabited homes steadily increases, CLTB will have to find ways to help residents to be fully in charge of managing their housing projects, while keeping them involved in the wider CLT movement.

In order to cope with these challenges, CLTB has entered into several agreements and has developed measures to increase its autonomy. Until recently, for example, CLTB has mainly worked with large, publicly-sponsored housing organizations such as the Housing

Fund in managing its construction projects, but CLTB has decided to be in charge of its own construction management in the future. Naturally, this will create a whole new set of financial and organizational issues. CLTB will now have to finance and to staff building operations itself. Within its organization, a building division will have to be organised. Also, the double position of simultaneously being a builder and a community organizer can be challenging, especially when problems occur during the building process.

Next, CLTB has recently made efforts to attract private donors and investors to finance its operations. In 2017, for the first time, the organization started a fundraising campaign. This led to a few important gifts by private charity foundations a year later. CLTB wants to expand this practice in the near future by creating a land cooperative. Such a cooperative would enable civil investors to invest their money in the acquisition of community land for affordable housing and spaces for social, cultural, and economic activities. Alongside the Public Utility Foundation, which purchases land through grants and donations, CLTB's cooperative would purchase land with its shareholders' investments. Such a cooperative would not only increase CLTB's capacity and autonomy; it would also enable CLTB to diversify its production — for instance, by integrating rental units into its projects and by helping social and cultural projects to gain access to affordable land.

Furthermore, CLTB has worked hard to expand and to strengthen the larger CLT movement within Brussels, across Belgium, and in neighboring countries. By disseminating the model more widely, CLTB hopes more individuals and organizations will become active defenders of the community land trust. Since the very beginning of CLTB, its initiators have been making the case for CLTs in the rest of Belgium and Europe. Several conferences have been organized in Brussels, where invited guests from the UK and the USA have presented their work. At these gatherings, the foundation for an informal network among European activists, practitioners, and academics interested in the CLT model was laid. Later on, CLTB staff and board members have been regularly presenting their work. They helped the CLT in Ghent to take its first steps toward becoming established. After visiting CLTB, a busload of city officials, politicians, and legal experts from Lille (France) were convinced to adopt the model as well. This precipitated the enactment in France of national legislation enabling the establishment of CLTs (*Organismes de Foncier Solidaire*, OFS) and led to the creation of the country's first CLT, initiated by the municipal government in Lille. CLTB has also taken the initiative in bringing together urban CLTs from the northwest of Europe by starting Sustainable Housing for Inclusive and Cohesive Cities (SHICC), a project aimed at promoting further dissemination of the CLT model throughout Europe.[22]

> CLTB has taken the initiative in promoting further dissemination of the CLT model throughout Europe.

IV. (IN)CONCLUSION

CLTB has succeeded in building a solid operation in a relatively short period of time. Several precipitating or sustaining factors allowed this to happen: the CLTB network, composed of community organizations, neighborhood groups and housing activists; a housing policy traditionally paying great attention to homeownership, providing a favorable regime for developing owner-occupied CLT homes; new public budgets for affordable housing; the lagging construction of social housing; and the regional government's willingness to invest in socially innovative alternatives in the housing market. Another prerequisite for CLTB's success was the basic mentality of CLTB's initiators, members, and leaders, which has hovered between lobbying for their core values while implementing them with a level of pragmatism.

First, expanding and maintaining a broad network of both associations and public bodies has been essential. The close collaboration with a professional social housing organization such as the Brussels Housing Fund and with local community organizations, for example, was very important for developing the first real estate operations and for shaping the CLT community. CLTB's commitment to disseminate the model and to support start-up groups elsewhere also contributed to its own success, when CLTs in other cities and countries began referring to Brussels as an example worth emulating.

Second, CLTB's initiators have negotiated firmly to ensure the autonomy of the organization and to have residents and civil society represented on the board of directors.

Third, the organization has been relying on step-by-step problem-solving. The feasibility study that formed the basis for founding the CLTB more or less described the organization that is starting to take shape today. To get there, numerous obstacles had to be overcome, while almost all CLT components had to be (re)invented and adapted to the Brussels legal and political context. Today, for instance, now that more and more homes are becoming occupied, much thought is being given to how CLTB can help residents to manage their condominiums.

Although CLTB has succeeded in operationalizing the CLT model in the Brussels Capital Region and in developing several successful housing projects, the organization is today facing significant challenges in going to scale. In the years ahead, CLTB will have to diversify its resources, attracting private investors and donors. It will have to strengthen its regional legislative framework to ensure continued regional support. It will have to create the internal capacity and expertise to fiscally optimize the construction of new projects. New competences within the organization, such as project development and condominium management support, will have to be developed. CLTB must also be diligent in protecting its autonomy despite its dependency on governmental funding, while preserving the predominant role of residents and civil society in governing the organization. The staff, board, and membership of CLTB will have to be steadfast in continuing to advocate for the central position of *community* within a community land trust.

> Such advocacy does not aim to replace the social housing policy that already exists, but to supplement it.

Beyond dealing with these many issues, CLTB hopes to work with its allies inside and outside of government to structurally embed some key CLT principles into the government's regular housing policy and spatial policy, including: non-speculative land use; permanent affordability of publicly subsidized homeownership; and community participation in the development of affordable housing and in the governance of the organizations doing development. Such advocacy does not aim to *replace* the social housing policy that already exists, but to *supplement* it, making the general housing policy in Brussels and in Belgium more equitable, inclusive, and sustainable. Ultimately, CLTB aims to disseminate the principle that lies at the heart of a community land trust, the principle that elevates the use value of real estate over its exchange value.

Ten years ago, a community land trust in Brussels was still an utopian idea, a distant dream of a small number of activists and community workers. Today, Community Land Trust Brussels is firmly established. The organisation has removed from the Brussels real estate market the first small pieces of land, colouring in the first pieces of a map where other rules apply. There is still a lot of work to be done before this unique approach to integrating resident participation into the design and operation of permanently affordable housing on land that is community-owned becomes mainstream. But CLTB is ready and eager to accept the challenge.

Fig. 6.5. CLTB staff, 2018. ANTOINE MEYER

Notes

1. After West London, Luxembourg, and Hamburg.

2. The so-called "At Risk of Poverty or Social Exclusion" (AROPE), an indicator developed in the framework of the Europe 2020 strategy, measures the share of people that meets at least one of the following conditions: 1) the household's disposable income is below the national poverty risk limit; 2) is between 0 and 59 years old and lives in a family with a very Low Work Intensity (LWI); 3) is in Severe Material Deprivation (SMD).

3. This means they have a foreign nationality, they are born with a foreign nationality, or one of their parents has a foreign nationality.

4. The term "poor crescent" refers to the crescent-shaped sequence of neighbourhoods marked by a concentration of poverty indicators.

5. In 1989, the federal government of Belgium delegated housing policy to the regions of Brussels, Flanders, and Wallonia. This has been part of a larger federalization process, in which different former federal state domains were transferred to the regions.

6. The Brussels Capital Region has only recently abolished the housing bonus, a tax reduction for homeowners. It has replaced this measure by registration fee reduction, whereby all registration fees are waived on the first 175,000 EUR of a real estate purchase (Art. 46bis of Brussels-Capital Region's Registration, Mortgage, and Clerk's Office Fees Code).

7. Cheap loans are offered by the Brussels Housing Fund, a subsidized organization that also develops rental and owner-occupied housing for households with a low and modest income.

8. Thanks to regional support, Citydev.brussels, a "regional development company," develops homes and sells them to middle-income households for only two-thirds of their market value. In addition, the buyer can buy the property with a reduced VAT rate of 6%.

9. This information is explicitly mentioned on the Citydev-website: *https://www.citydev. brussels/nl/onze-filosofie.*

10. Between 2001 and 2011, the proportion of homeowners in the BCR fell from 42.7% to 38.81% (CENSUS 2011).

11. The Belgians who participated in this study visit were Michel Renard, from the Municipality of Molenbeek, Loïc Géronnez from Periferia, Geert De Pauw from Community Centre Bonnevie, and Thomas Dawance, researcher. Geert and Thomas later became part of CLTB's first staff.

12. For more on this dynamic, see: *http://www.periferia.be/Bibliomedia/PUB/EP2011/periferia_2011_construire_politique_publique.pdf.*

13. The Brussels Housing Code includes all instruments and measures of the housing policy in the Brussels Capital Region.

14. For several CLTB projects, the Brussels Housing Fund, a subsidized organization that also develops rental and owner-occupied housing for households with a low and modest income, has acted as the building's developer.

15. Each year, the European Union launches "Urban Innovative Actions," supporting the development of innovative and participative projects around Europe that address urban challenges. Urban authorities, together with key stakeholders such as agencies, associations, private sector organisations, research institutions and NGOs are eligible to submit proposals.

16. Interestingly, Louvain-la-Neuve will be one of the first Belgian cities, after Brussels and Ghent, to start a community land trust. After being elected in 2018, the new mayor launched a plan for building 140 CLT homes, as part of a bigger new sustainable neighbourhood.

17. In French, Association Sans But Lucratif (ASBL).

18. In French, Fondation d'Utilité Public, a non-profit entity different from an ASBL, mainly used for the management of assets. One of the important differences between them is that a Foundation doesn't have members, making it very difficult to implement the CLT governance principles. CLTB resolved this issue by determining that board members of the Foundation would be designated by the members of the ASBL.

19. The representatives of the first two groups are elected by the NGO's general assembly. The government representatives are designated by the government, and approved by the assembly. Members of the Foundation's board are designated by the members of the ASBL, thus guaranteeing a strong link between both entities.

20. For the first projects, these groups were composed at the moment CLTB purchased land, thus enabling the future residents to have a say in the content of the public tender for an architectural project. Because of the long process in building any project, this meant that groups were composed 5 to 6 years before the residents could move into their homes. Today, groups are composed later on in the process, once the building permit is obtained, reducing the preparation period for homeowners to 2 or 3 years, if all goes well.

21. The vast majority of potential buyers have a migrant background, with a predominance of people with roots in Guinea, Morocco, and Congo. Furthermore, most of the families have a very modest income or benefit from a replacement income.

22. SHICC is a three-year initiative funded by the European Union. CLT Brussels, CLT Ghent, the London CLT, and the Lille CLT are SHICC's founding members.

References

Aernouts, N. and Ryckewaert, M. (2017). "Beyond housing: On the role of commoning in the establishment of a Community Land Trust project," *International Journal of Housing Policy* 18 (4), 503–521.

Aernouts, N., Ryckewaert, M. van Heur, B., and Moritz, B. (2017). *Housing the social. Investigating the role of commoning in the development of social housing initiatives.* Unpublished doctoral thesis.

De Pauw, G. (2011). *Passieve woningen, actieve bewoners* (Brussels: Opbouwwerk).

Dessouroux, C., Bensliman, R., Bernard, N., De Laet, S., Demonty, F., Marissal, P. and Surkyn, J. (2016). "Huisvesting in Brussel: diagnose en uitdagingen," *Brussels Studies* 99, 1–32.

Englert, M., Luyten, S., Fele, D., Mazina, D., Mendes Da Costa, E. and Missinne, S. for Commission Communautaire Commune (2018). *Welzijnsbarometer 2018.* Brussels: Observatoire de la santé et du social.

Geurts, V. and Goossens, L. (2004). "Home ownership and social inequality in Belgium." (In K. Kurz and H.P. Blossfeld. *Home Ownership and Social Inequality in Comparative Perspective,* Stanford, California: Stanford University Press, 79–113.

Loopmans, M. and Kesteloot, C. (2009). "Social inequalities." *Brussels Studies* 16, 1–12.

Romainville, A. (2010). "Who benefits from home ownership support?" *Brussels Studies* 34, 1–20.

Vermeulen, S. (2009). *Needed: an intelligent and integrated vision for Brussels' urban planning.* Paper presented at the 4th International Conference of the International Forum on Urbanism (IFoU), Amsterdam/Delft.

7.

Lands in Trust for Urban Farming
Toward a Scalable Model

Nate Ela and Greg Rosenberg

In cities around the world, people are looking to urban agriculture for a wide range of benefits, from providing fresh food and supporting healthy eating habits to teaching job skills and offering access to nature. Urban farms are increasingly seen as a possible engine for economic development, whether as the main source of income for full-time farmers, growing the raw materials for value-added products, or supplementary income for growers who hold other jobs. Community supported agriculture[1] (CSA) farms can be a good fit for urban settings, bringing the farm into close proximity to the membership. And finally, community gardens are a particularly compelling application of urban agriculture, making land available to residents of neighborhoods where access to fresh, healthy food is limited — or nonexistent.

None of this can happen, however, without land on which to grow crops.[2] A wide range of people — from individual growers to mentors, foundation officials, university researchers, urban planners, and policy makers who would like to see urban farms succeed — have been grappling with questions related to land. Which models of tenure are best suited to securing access to land for urban farming? Which models are most effective in preserving access and affordability over time? Which models are most efficient in allocating scarce resources, while also promoting equity and engagement with community residents who will be an urban farm's neighbors and customers?

The high cost of urban land relative to rural land poses a major problem for would-be urban farmers. Unlike rural farmers, they are competing for land with many other potential uses, which creates inflationary pressures on land prices. In Wisconsin, for example, rents for rural cropland averaged $140 per acre in 2018 (USDA, 2018). This is a small fraction of the price an urban farmer would pay for an acre of tillable land at market rates in Chicago or other cities. Yet, food grown in cities must remain price-competitive with food grown in rural areas. Few if any crops can be sold at prices that would cover the higher land costs, and urban growers cannot simply add a premium to reflect the value of the contributions they make to their neighborhoods.

If affordable land is key to commercially viable, community-engaged urban farming, the question becomes how to protect affordability over the long term. This means ensuring that urban farms — and community gardens — are not displaced by rapidly rising prices in a speculative real estate market, while ensuring that land is not allocated haphazardly in neighborhoods where values may be stagnant or declining. In both cases, the struggle is how to ensure space is available for agricultural projects that are rooted in and beneficial to surrounding communities.

> People are looking to land trusts to hold land for urban farms and community gardens.

Over the last several decades, housing and environmental advocates have developed land trust models to ensure that community priorities for the use of land are not displaced by speculative market forces. Open space and conservation land trusts have focused on protecting ecologically valuable land at the urban fringe. Community land trusts have sought to preserve housing affordability and security of tenure in cities and suburbs. These models are increasingly being brought to bear on the challenge of providing and protecting land for urban agriculture.

PROGRAM DESIGN — EIGHT STRATEGIC QUESTIONS REGARDING LANDHOLDING FOR URBAN FARMS

1. Who Should Be the Landholding Entity?

Different types of entities could hold land for urban agriculture, including government agencies, land banks, agriculture cooperatives, or even private firms. Cities have large amounts of unused acreage owned by churches, corporate headquarters, educational institutions, and public agencies that may be appropriate for urban agriculture. Cities such as Oakland, California; Portland, Oregon; Madison, Wisconsin; and Philadelphia, Pennsylvania have conducted inventories to determine where such opportunities exist.

However, increasingly around the United States, people are looking to land trusts as an entity that is well-suited to holding land for urban farms and community gardens. When considering whether a land trust should hold title to land or, instead, should manage lands held by public entities, property tax issues are an important consideration. Market-value property tax assessments can make land unaffordable, even for a nonprofit land trust. (For this reason, the Athens Land Trust in Athens, Georgia opted not to own urban farmland; unfavorable property tax treatment would have yielded a full market-value assessment for the land, despite the long-term restrictions placed on it.)

2. How Will the Landholder Relate to Community Members?

Whether land is held by a nonprofit land trust, a government agency, or some other entity, the relationship between the landholder and community members will be a key question. Are community members included as board members of a land trust and, if so, how? Are they consulted by public officials, if the land is held by a city agency or county land bank, and if so, how?

3. How Will Land Be Made Affordable?

If urban farmers are to have any hope of sustained success, their cost to access land should be roughly on par with that of rural farmers. Thus, one reasonable target for affordability would be for urban farmers to devote the same percentage of the cost of access to land as rural farmers do. For rural farmers, this proportion will depend on the main crop that is being grown, whereas urban farmers will be more likely to have a more intensive and diversified growing strategy.

4. How Will Land Be Used?

What type of land is appropriate depends on how growers plan to use it. Will they grow in greenhouses, hoop houses, or outdoors? Will they be growing flowers, herbs, or vegetables? Will they set up composting facilities? Land use will also depend not only on growers' desires, but on zoning and other regulations.

5. Who Will Be the Growers?

Again, a land tenure model must be responsive to different types of growers. These types include job trainees working on nonprofit urban farms, new commercial growers testing their business models on incubator farms, independent commercial growers with just a few years or decades of experience, and noncommercial community gardeners who are growing food for their own consumption. A tenure model can also help encourage community-engaged urban agriculture by minority-run firms, and by prioritizing access to land for farmers who will grow in their own neighborhood.

6. How Will Land Be Conveyed to Growers?

Although this is the central question to be answered by a land tenure model, we do not expect there to be a single answer. Land may be secured differently for growers with different purposes and with different levels of experience. Before securing land for particular farmers, however, there is the question of how to protect land for agricultural use. This could mean transferring publicly or privately owned land into a land trust, which then provides leases to individual farmers or to an urban farming organization.

It makes sense to have different terms for different types of farmers. Nonprofit urban farms could be eligible for long-term leases—perhaps 99-year renewable leases for the most well-established organizations. Such leases would ensure long-term agricultural use and provide security to urban farms committed to being an ongoing resource for a neighborhood. For individual farmers, a renewable short-term lease could have performance measures negotiated by the farmer and the leasing entity, with input from community members. Farmers could thus work their way into long-term security of tenure by demonstrating their ability to pay the (below-market) rent and provide community benefits.

7. What Type of Support Will Growers Need to Be Successful?

Support will vary widely based on the experience of the farmers, issues relating to the land, and challenges in accessing the local market for their produce. For land-related issues, farmers may need support for soil remediation, installation of infrastructure (water and electricity), construction of agricultural buildings, negotiating favorable property tax assessments if they are the landowners, and zoning changes in some cases. Again, the support of a team of people and organizations is usually required to address all these issues.

8. How is Success Defined? What Expectations Are Realistic?

In defining a system for land tenure, people must grapple with what a successful urban farming sector looks like. Although nonprofit urban farms have been demonstrably effective, most cities have not seen many small, for-profit urban farms that have created well-paying jobs. If communities or government officials expect urban farms to be a major vehicle for near-term job creation, those expectations may be unrealistic.

A successful land tenure model should support land remaining in agricultural use over a long period of time, so that urban farmers can test out for-profit and nonprofit business models. It will take time for farmers to learn which business models provide an acceptable mix of economic return and community benefits. Along the way, some farms will fail. This is normal with small businesses; the Small Business Association (2012) has found that only about half of small businesses survive the first five years. Rather than taking such failures as a sign that land should not be preserved for agricultural use, a successful land tenure model would quickly provide access to a new grower.

THE ROLE OF LAND TRUSTS IN PROVIDING AND PROTECTING AFFORDABLE LAND FOR URBAN FARMING

As in other areas of community development, the nonprofit sector has a special role to play in kick-starting urban farming.[3] Urban agriculture is a relatively low-cost approach to job creation and neighborhood revitalization, compared to other forms of revitalization. An urban farm can be built more quickly and cheaply than housing or mixed-use development. In practice, of course, the fact that business models for urban farming are

Urban agriculture is a relatively low-cost approach to job creation and neighborhood revitalization.

still being tested means delays are often encountered in raising capital and satisfying regulatory requirements.

Over the past thirty years, the land trust has emerged in the United States as a preferred model for holding land for community gardens and urban farms. This reflects the convergence of two trends: the creation of specialized open space land trusts to conserve land for community gardens, and the moves that some community land trusts (CLTs) have made to promote urban agriculture.

There is a distinction between open space land trusts and community land trusts. Open space land trusts — which may also be called conservation land trusts – focus on the protection and preservation of lands on which are built few (if any) residential structures and which are not being productively used to grow food or fiber. Open space land trusts, moreover, do not generally have an organizational structure that fosters community-based governance.[4] Community land trusts, by contrast, acquire and hold land for the benefit of a place-based community to which the organization is accountable. They generally have a tripartite board structure that includes seats dedicated to beneficiaries of the trust (usually people who live in housing held by the trust), residents from neighboring communities, and people with needed expertise or organizational connections.

Under both types of land trust, a nonprofit organization owns or holds rights to use parcels of land, but leases out parcels of land for productive use. The size of the lease fees will depend on what is needed to cover the lessor's costs of holding the land and paying for its own administrative overhead, some of which may be subsidized through public or private philanthropy.

Open Space Land Trusts:
New York Community Garden Land Trusts

In 1999, the administration of New York City Mayor Rudolph Giuliani announced a plan to auction off over one hundred pieces of city-owned land that were home to community gardens. Gardeners and their allies mobilized in resistance to the plan, organizing demonstrations and filing lawsuits (Brooklyn Queens Land Trust, n.d.). In 2002, after a negotiated settlement of the lawsuits with Mayor Michael Bloomberg's administration, sixty-nine gardens were purchased by the Trust for Public Lands (TPL). The New York Restoration Project (NYRP), a nonprofit founded and funded by the singer Bette Midler, took ownership of dozens more gardens.

In the years since, TPL has established three local land trusts to hold and manage the gardens: the Manhattan Land Trust, the Brooklyn Queens Land Trust, and the Bronx Land Trust. The board of each land trust is a mix of community garden leaders and staff from New York City nonprofit organizations. NYRP has now taken on a broader mission to provide green space to underserved areas of the city, and is being led by a range of New

York philanthropists, businesspeople, and civic leaders. At some of its sites, the amount of space available for community-managed gardens has been reduced in favor of tidy pocket parks (New York Restoration Project, n.d.).

Community Land Trusts

Since the 1980s, community land trusts in the United States have had a primary focus on permanently affordable housing, but there has also been a parallel, albeit less common, focus on agricultural practices, both in rural and urban settings. Especially in the last decade, CLTs have played three roles in support of urban agriculture. First, some CLTs formed to provide affordable housing have begun to hold land for community gardens and urban farms. Second, some housing-focused CLTs have provided programmatic support for urban agriculture, rather than taking on ownership of agricultural land themselves. Also, a few organizations focused exclusively on urban agriculture have been founded and structured as community land trusts, adapting some of the organizational and operational features of CLTs that develop housing.

Fig. 7.1. Troy Gardens in Madison, Wisconsin, an award-wining project combining affordable housing and urban agriculture, developed by the Madison Area Community Land Trust.[5]

Here we focus on several applications of the CLT model to urban agriculture, starting with the Southside Community Land Trust, which remains the only CLT in the USA with a sole focus on preserving land for community gardens and urban farms.

Southside Community Land Trust

Southside Community Land Trust (Southside CLT, n.d.) holds title to sixteen community gardens in Providence, Rhode Island. Southside CLT provides programmatic support (such as arranging for bulk purchases of organic fertilizers) for these gardens, as well as for the twenty-five gardens in its network that are owned by other organizations. Southside differs from other community land trusts in that it only holds land for gardens and farms rather than for affordable housing. However, like traditional CLTs, it has built community representation and engagement into its governance structure. Fifty-one percent of its board members must be elected directly from the gardeners (Yuen, 2012: 36–37).

In addition to protecting land for community gardens, Southside CLT manages two commercial farms. City Farm is a three-quarter-acre commercial urban farm in south Providence that began in 1986. Urban Edge Farm is a fifty-acre farm in nearby Cranston, Rhode Island; its mission is to support seven new farmers who collaboratively manage the land (Southside CLT). The land for Urban Edge was purchased by the state in 2002, pursuant to the state's Open Space Preservation Act (Rhode Island Department of Environmental Management, n.d.). The site, which was formerly a dairy farm, is now owned

Fig. 7.2. Southside Community Land Trust, Providence, Rhode Island.

and protected by the Rhode Island Department of Environmental Management, which leases it to Southside CLT for one dollar per year (ibid.; Ewert, 2012: 97). About twenty of the fifty acres are cultivable.

Southside CLT initially operated its own CSA farm at Urban Edge Farm, but within a few years it became clear that production would not cover the significant staffing costs (Ewert, 2012: 91). Through Urban Edge Farm, Southside CLT now teaches farming practices to new farmers, rents them farm equipment, provides compost and fertilizer, and plows the land once a year (Snowden, 2006). After going through training, these beginning farmers can rent up to two acres of land at below-market rates. These farming businesses are owned and operated by people who have experience in farming, but weren't able to buy or rent land on their own at market rates. They sell through CSAs, directly to institutions, and through growers' cooperatives.

Athens Land Trust

As an adjunct to its affordable housing and land conservation efforts, the Athens Land Trust (ALT) in Athens, Georgia has made a deep commitment to community agriculture programming as a strategy for community engagement and neighborhood revitalization. The three-fold mission of their Community Agriculture Program is (a) to promote sustainable agriculture, (b) to increase access to healthy food, and (c) to support economic and entrepreneurial opportunities for underserved youth and adults. This Program has five components:

Fig. 7.3. Athens Land Trust, West Broad farmers market, Athens, Georgia.

1. *Community Garden Network:* The CGN is a partnership among organizations that grow and promote school and community garden projects.

2. *Farm to School:* ALT is working with the local school system to expand school gardens and to incorporate fresh food grown on school grounds into cafeteria meals.

3. *Vendor Development:* The West Broad Farmers Market provides retail space for underserved farmers and small business owners.

4. *Young Urban Farmers:* In partnership with the Clarke County School District, ALT established the Young Urban Farmers program in order to provide underserved high school students with sustainable agriculture education, hands-on work experience, and leadership development.

5. *Farmer Outreach:* This program is a collaborative effort with the Natural Resources Conservation Service to conduct outreach and educational activities for underserved groups in northeast Georgia.

Oakland Community Land Trust

The programming of the Oakland Community Land Trust in Oakland, California is focused on three core initiatives: residential anti-displacement; career pathways/construction training; and land access for food production. In their Urban Agriculture and Community Gardens program, they are building an administrative and legal capacity to acquire and to steward land in perpetuity for a variety of open space, agricultural, and gardening uses that directly serve low-income families and neighborhoods. They are collaborating with community partners to reuse blighted, tax-defaulted parcels in ways that engage existing neighborhood residents in the production of healthy food.

The Oakland Community Land Trust is currently in the process of acquiring a number of tax-defaulted and lien-burdened parcels from Alameda County. Once taking ownership, the land will be prepared for community use, with long-term ground leases provided to partner organizations for urban agriculture initiatives.

THE CENTRAL SERVER MODEL—
A SCALABLE APPROACH TO URBAN FARMING?

The "central server" is a model developed within the community land trust movement to facilitate the scaling and stewardship of permanently affordable housing on a regional or city-wide basis, while striking a balance between local control and centralized services. The model was introduced in 2009 in Atlanta, and proposed soon thereafter in New Orleans.[6] Supporters hoped to spur the growth of neighborhood-based community land trusts

> A central server could do the "heavy lifting" that is beyond the ability of small, neighborhood-based organizations.

by creating a central entity that would provide a variety of technical services, including: accounting, development, and real estate transactions; negotiating with funders and lenders; and managing resales — all of which require more expertise than a neighborhood-based organization can easily muster.

From the experiences in Atlanta and New Orleans, affordable housing advocates soon learned that the burdens placed on a central server can be difficult to bear from a legal, political, financial, and community relations perspective. There is not the space in this chapter to evaluate the effectiveness of the central server model for affordable housing,[7] but it is worth noting that affordable-housing CLTs in a number of cities in the United States are continuing to explore the best ways to design and to fund a regional operation serving multiple CLTs in multiple neighborhoods.[8]

In the context of urban farming, where transactions are more straightforward because they do not involve housing or residents, we believe that a central server model may hold significant promise. Successfully implementing such a model in the urban farming context, as it does in the housing context, would depend on striking a balance between local control and centralized economies of scale. An appropriate architecture would involve a web of neighborhood-based "satellite" organizations served by a citywide organization, the "central server." The central server would provide a suite of services for the satellites and for the farmers to whom the satellites provide land.

Possible Roles of a Central Server in an Urban Farming Context

A central server could do the "heavy lifting" that is beyond the ability of small, neighborhood-based organizations that are necessarily focused on starting up urban farming projects. With expertise in land use and real estate transactions, a central server could negotiate with local government to secure publicly owned land for agriculture, obtain favorable tax treatment, and gain access to city services to provide needed infrastructure to gardens and farms. In addition, a central server could help to provide training and technical support to satellite organizations. Providing such services in group settings would be less costly, and would create opportunities to build connections between satellite organizations.

A central server could also provide a single point of connection to funders. This would increase the collective leverage of neighborhood organizations beyond what they could accomplish individually, and reduce overhead for funders by packaging what might otherwise be numerous similar grant applications. (Of course, satellite organizations may also seek funding for their own operations.) A central server would also have access to officials and decision-making in city government that is beyond the reach of smaller organizations.

The term *server* is key to understanding the model. A central server would exist to serve satellite entities in each of the neighborhoods encompassed by the central server. The staff for a central server would have to be skilled at "playing well with others" and studiously avoid engaging in turf battles or picking favorites. This would not be easy, especially in cities where local elected officials have a strong say in how projects are developed in their districts.

Roles of Neighborhood-Based Satellites in a Central Server for Urban Farming

Satellite organizations would serve as the voice of their community. They may be existing nonprofits (community development corporations, community land trusts, etc.), new start-ups, or more informal entities. No matter what form they take, they should be able to speak credibly on behalf of their neighborhoods and ensure that land use decisions are in the best interest of residents.

A central server would free neighborhood-based satellite organizations from the heavy lifting of real estate transactions, infrastructure installation, and negotiating favorable property tax treatment. Satellites would then be able to focus on the critical work of managing productive land with the oversight and engagement of neighborhood residents, through participatory planning and recruiting growers who are committed to integrating farming into the fabric of their community.

Satellite entities would have to play some governance role in the central server. This would help to ensure that the central server's staff would keep their eyes on the prize of supporting neighborhood organizations.

Who Should Own the Land in a Central Server Model?

In an urban agriculture context, it would likely make more sense for the central server to be the landholding entity. As described below, this is the approach that NeighborSpace has used to great success in Chicago. It takes advantage of economies of scale and real estate expertise, and provides a single point of contact for public agencies that provide land for farms and gardens.

On the other hand, satellite organizations may want to own the land themselves to secure better local control over neighborhood development. A "hybrid" approach might also work, where the land was initially owned by the central server, but satellite organizations would have the option to purchase lands in their neighborhood once they had built a management and stewardship capacity locally. Such a hybrid approach might also provide that, in the event a satellite organization failed, lands would revert to the central server.

NeighborSpace: A Central Server Case Study

NeighborSpace is the closest existing organization to what might be considered a central-server land trust model for urban agriculture. Founded to help conserve Chicago's community gardens, the land trust has recently begun to hold land for commercially oriented urban farms as well. Its history and structure point toward how a central server model might be further developed in other cities.[9]

NeighborSpace was founded in 1996 as a response to a city planning report that found Chicago lagging behind other major cities in terms of open space per capita (City of Chicago et al., 1998). The report noted that some of the city's 55,000 vacant lots had been converted or appropriated for neighborhood uses, including community gardens. Yet even as development threatened many of these gardens, no public agency was tasked with conserving community-managed open space.

The report recommended creating a citywide land trust to hold urban gardens. In response, the City of Chicago, the Cook County Forest Preserve, and the Chicago Park District joined to found and to fund NeighborSpace, which would officially be an independent nonprofit (Chicago City Council, 1996). NeighborSpace has continued to operate with support and oversight from these three governmental entities, each of which provides $100,000 in annual funding, with each appointing two representatives to serve on the land trust's board of directors. The remaining three seats are reserved for non-governmental representatives.

As of mid-2019, NeighborSpace owned or leased 115 sites. Although accounting for only a fraction of the hundreds of community gardens in Chicago (Taylor and Lovell, 2012), NeighborSpace nevertheless protects a sizable amount of land: 26.4 acres of green space, the equivalent of fifteen football pitches.

NeighborSpace takes on many of the roles of a central server while leaving certain other roles to community organizations. Community gardens are managed by groups of gardeners, while NeighborSpace takes on vital and often costly tasks that would prove burdensome for individual groups of gardeners, including:

- Acquiring land;

- Securing title;

- Completing environmental testing and remediation;

- Securing liability insurance;

- Applying for property tax exemptions;

- Arranging for water access; and

- Responding to stewardship emergencies like fallen trees.

Fig. 7.4. Drake Garden, built by residents on an empty lot in the Albany Park neighborhood, Chicago, Illinois.

> NeighborSpace's ownership also ensures that public investments will continue to benefit the public.

NeighborSpace is careful, however, to leave community organizing to community organizations. Before it will consider securing title to a community garden, the land trust requires a community partner to take responsibility, along with at least three garden leaders and at least ten community stakeholders (Helphand, 2015: 2). NeighborSpace also leaves the governance and management of gardens to community partners, so long as they meet minimum insurance requirements.

Around 2010, NeighborSpace began holding land for urban farms (Ela, 2016). This happened after Growing Home, a successful nonprofit urban farm, saw an opportunity to expand onto a nearby city-owned parcel. Rather than seeking to have the city transfer ownership directly, the farm sought to have the city transfer the land to NeighborSpace, which would then lease the land to Growing Home.

For NeighborSpace, holding land for commercial farming was a new proposition. After considering the issue, the land trust's directors agreed that supporting urban farms fit with the mission of preserving community-managed open space. In addition to requiring that farms be operated by not-for-profit entities, NeighborSpace disallows any permanent structures (hoop-houses are permissible), and ensures that a farm's size is suited to the neighborhood context.

From the city's perspective, NeighborSpace's ownership of land being used for urban agriculture solves several problems. The land trust can help coordinate and raise funds for environmental testing and remediation, expenses that can run to several hundred thousand dollars. NeighborSpace's ownership also ensures that, if a particular gardening group dissolves or if an urban farming organization ceases operations, public investments will continue to benefit the public.

This new model has expanded. In the West Side neighborhood of East Garfield Park, NeighborSpace now leases 2.6 acres to Chicago FarmWorks, a nonprofit farm that sells its produce at wholesale prices to the Greater Chicago Food Depository (Heartland Alliance, 2012). Beyond these two sites, officials from city agencies and local foundations have come to see NeighborSpace as a useful tool for expanding Chicago's commercial agriculture sector.

NeighborSpace is the organization closest to what a central server might look like. But the point is not that its model should simply be adopted in other cities. The conditions surrounding the founding and funding of NeighborSpace are unique to Chicago. Elsewhere, urban farming organizations might need to spearhead a process to create a new land tenure model and might need support from local foundations, rather than government partners. That could produce a more formalized network of community-controlled, neighborhood-level satellite organizations than exists in Chicago. NeighborSpace provides a helpful example, but the structure of new urban farming land trusts will surely vary, depending on the contexts and resources available in different cities.

Best Practices for Designing a Central Server

- *Encourage government buy-in.* The vast majority of land for urban farming will likely come from the public sector. In addition, public subsidies for remediation and operations will often be needed. As a *quid pro quo*, government may seek to control the central server's functions. A central server will work best, however, when government has a voice, but not a veto.

- *Engage with communities.* Community engagement in the guidance and governance of the central server will be important for growers, consumers, and neighbors to support the central server and to work cooperatively with the central server in managing land for urban agriculture.

- *Establish a clear division of roles and responsibilities.* There should be a clear division of roles and responsibilities between the central server and neighborhood-based satellites, as well as between the central server and government, community organizations, and farmers.

■ *Land should be owned by the central server.* Land ownership by the central server will generally work best, but there may be an option for local entities to eventually purchase lands in their own neighborhoods (with reversion to the central server if the satellite goes under).

■ *Central server should do the technical work.* The central server should attend to legal and financial issues that require technical expertise beyond that of growers. Such expertise includes title, insurance, land preparation, construction of infrastructure, and property taxation.

■ *Central server should foster communication and education.* The central server should be transparent in its own policies, operations and finances, while encouraging communication among growers, sharing information about best farming practices.

■ *Central server should seek favorable property tax treatment.* To protect the ongoing affordability of urban farmland, the central server should look for opportunities to reduce or to stabilize property taxes on its holdings.[10]

CONCLUSION

Farms and gardens are hardly a new feature of America's urban landscapes, having repeatedly cropped up and withered away since the late 1800s (Lawson, 2005). This coming and going frames a puzzle: how might urban agriculture become, and remain, a permanent part of our cities? How might we reimagine and restructure land tenure to help urban farmers contribute on a long-term basis to the health (and perhaps the wealth) of the cities and communities in which they grow?

Answers to these questions are emerging in fits and starts, as people tinker with ways that urban farmers can gain access to land on a long-term basis. In all likelihood, no single dominant model will emerge; instead, we will see the development of a diverse mix of strategies, including the increasing use of land trusts.

We have proposed, in this chapter, a way in which current strategies — the central server model, in particular — might be extended and expanded to help urban farmers and community gardeners to become more securely rooted in their communities. Community ownership of land, combined with long-term ground leases, offers a tried and true approach that provides security of tenure for urban growers, while preserving the community's voice in land use decisions. We hope this approach will prove fruitful, grafting onto, hybridizing with, and fertilizing ongoing efforts to expand urban agriculture in the United States and in other countries as well.

Notes

1. Community-supported agriculture (CSA model) is a system that connects producers and consumers within the food system more closely by allowing consumers to subscribe to the harvest of a certain farm or group of farms. It is an alternative socioeconomic model of agriculture and food distribution that allows the producer and consumer to share the risks of farming.

2. Although urban agriculture takes a wide range of forms, we focus here on land tenure models that can best support ground-based, outdoor growing of commercial crops. Such growing practices, compared to growing on rooftops or indoors, are more likely to yield the full range of community benefits mentioned above. Also, because community non-profit organizations or individual growers may have less access to capital than rooftop or indoor growers, the cost and availability of land is an even more pressing constraint.

3. It is certainly possible for entities other than nonprofits to serve as landholding entities. Here we focus on the role of nonprofits both for reasons of space and because the non-profit form is often adopted in situations where there is "at least one class of patrons for whom both the costs of contracting and the costs of ownership are quite high" (Hansmann, 1996: 228), meaning that vesting ownership in a single group can result in severe inefficiencies. Here, government entities and potential donors would face significant contracting costs if they were to retain ownership of land and to contract with individual growers.

4. There is movement in this direction, however. Openlands, the regional open space land trust in Chicago and its environs, is focused on the ecological potential of farmland when used as a buffer for conservation lands. Also, the Trust for Public Lands has recently developed a "working lands" initiative (Trust for Public Lands, n.d.). Meanwhile, a move is under way in the open space land trust community to promote "community conservation" initiatives (Aldrich and Levy, 2015).

5. Community gardens and an urban farm were incorporated into the Troy Gardens project of the Madison Area Community Land Trust, alongside affordable housing. A case study of the project is available at *http://www.troygardens.net*

6. For more on the Atlanta model, see the web page of the Atlanta Land Trust (*https://atlantalandtrust.org*). It is also described in PD&R Edge (2012) and Schneggenburger (2011). The Crescent City Community Land Trust in New Orleans adopted a central server model on its founding in 2011 (Khanmalek, 2013).

7. For more information on how the CLT central server model has played out in Essex County, New Jersey, see DeFillipis (2012). A detailed examination of central server initiatives across the United States can be found in Baldwin (2016).

8. In 2015, a group of CLTs in Boston formed the Metro Boston Community Land Trust Network, exploring the possibility of Dudley Neighbors Inc. functioning as a central server. (See the DNI profile in the present volume.) Other "central server" initiatives are currently under development in Denver and New York City.

9. This case study draws upon an article by the executive director of NeighborSpace (Helphand, 2015).

10. In some cases, this may require the central server to agree to a long-term ground lease when accepting land from a public entity, instead of receiving title, trading a bit of control in exchange for lower taxes.

References

Aldrich, Rob, and Melissa Levy (2015). Assessing, Planning and Measuring Comunity Conservation Impact: A Tool for Land Trusts. Land Trust Alliance. Accessed November 24, 2015, at *http://www.landtrustalliance.org/publication/community-conservation-tool*.

Atlanta Land Trust (n.d.). Accessed November 24, 2015, at *https://atlantalandtrust.org*.

Baldwin, Ben (2016). Networked Community Land Trusts: An Analysis of Existing Models and Needs Assessment for the Greater Boston Community Land Trust Network. Unpublished Master's Thesis. Tufts University.

Brooklyn Queens Land Trust (n.d.). About BQLT. Accessed November 24, 2015, at *http://www.bqlt.org/About/*.

Chicago City Council (1996). Committee on Finance, Authorization for Execution of Intergovernmental Agreement with Chicago Park District and Forest Preserve District of Cook County for Establishment of "NeighborSpace." Accessed October 31, 2015, at *http://www.eatbettermovemore.org/sa/policies/pdftext/ChicagoNeighborSpace.pdf*.

City of Chicago, Chicago Park District and Forest Preserve District of Cook County (1998). CitySpace: An Open Space Plan for Chicago.

DeFillipis, James (2012). "New Research on the Fundamental Issues of Central Server CLTs," Available at: *https://impact.adobeconnect.com/_a1162566415/p69u9e9xyjg/?launcher=false&fcsContent=true&pbMode=normal*.

Ela, Nate (2016). "Urban Commons as Property Experiment: Mapping Chicago's Farms and Gardens." *Fordham Urban Law Journal* 43(2): 247–294.

Ewert, Brianna (2012). Incubating New Farmers. Master's Thesis, University of Montana. Accessed November 24, 2015, at *https://scholarworks.umt.edu/cgi/viewcontent.cgi?article=2165&context=etd*.

Growing Power (2013). Farmers for Chicago. Accessed October 29, 2015, at *https://www. chicago.gov/city/en/depts/mayor/press_room/press_releases/2013/march_2013/ mayor_emanuel_launchesnewfarmersforchicagonetworkforchicagourban.html.*

Hansmann, Henry (1996). *The Ownership of Enterprise.* Cambridge, MA: Harvard University Press.

Heartland Alliance (2012). Heartland Human Care Services Breaks Ground on West Side Urban Farm. Accessed October 29, 2015, at *https://www.heartlandalliance.org/ press_release/urban-farm/.*

Helphand, Ben (2015). Permanently Grassroots with NeighborSpace. *Cities and the Environment (CATE)* 8(2): Art.19. Accessed November 24, 2015, at *http://digitalcommons. lmu.edu/cate/vol8/iss2/19.*

Khanmalek, Azeen (2013). CCLT Investment Strategy. American Planning Association Louisiana Chapter, October 2013 Monthly Bulletin. Accessed November 24, 2015, at *https://sites.google.com/a/louisianaplanning.com/homebusiness/2010newsletter/ 2013-october.*

Lawson, Laura (2005). *City Bountiful: A Century of Community Gardening in America.* Berkeley: University of California Press.

New York Restoration Project (N.D.). Target East Harlem Community Garden. Accessed November 24, 2015, at *http://www.nyrp.org/green-spaces/garden-details/target-east-harlem-community-garden.*

PD&R Edge (2012). Community Land Trusts in Atlanta, Georgia: A Central Server Model. Accessed November 24, 2015, at *http://www.huduser.gov/portal/pdredge/pdr_edge_ inpractice_112312.html.*

Rhode Island Department of Environmental Management (N.D.). Forest Stewardship: Rhode Island Landowners Discover New Strategies in Forest Conservation. Accessed November 24, 2015, at *http://www.dem.ri.gov/programs/bnatres/forest/pdf/ forstew.pdf.*

Schneggenburger, Andy (2011). Bringing CLTs to Scale in Atlanta. *Shelterforce,* Feb. 7, 2011. Accessed November 24, 2015, at *http://www.shelterforce.org/article bringing_clts_ to_scale_in_atlanta/.*

Small Business Association (2012). Frequently Asked Questions About Small Business. Accessed November 24, 2015, at *http://www.sba.gov/sites/default/files/FAQ_ Sept_2012.pdf.*

Snowden, Mary (2006). Farm Profile: Pak Express Farm. Accessed November 24, 2015, at *http://www.farmfresh.org/food/farm.php?farm=766#profile.*

Southside Community Land Trust (N.D.). Urban Edge Farm. Accessed November 24, 2015, at *https://www.southsideclt.org/category/urban-edge-farm/.*

Taylor, John R., and Sarah Taylor Lovell (2012). Mapping public and private spaces of urban agriculture in Chicago through the analysis of high-resolution aerial images in Google Earth. *Landscape and Urban Planning* 108: 57–70.

Trust for Public Lands (n.d.). Working Lands. Accessed November 24, 2015, at *https://www.tpl.org/our-work/our-land-and-water/working-lands.*

USDA National Agricultural Statistics Service (2015). Quick Stats: Average Cropland Cash Rent by State. Accessed November 24, 2015, at *https://bit.ly/3clo1ei*

Yuen, Jeffrey (2012). Hybrid Vigor: An Analysis of Land Tenure Arrangements in Addressing Land Security for Urban Community Gardens. Master's Thesis, Columbia University.

8.

Community Land Trusts in Informal Settlements

Adapting Features of Puerto Rico's
Caño Martín Peña CLT to Address Land Insecurity
in the Favelas of Rio de Janeiro, Brazil

Tarcyla Fidalgo Ribeiro, Line Algoed,
María E. Hernández-Torrales, Lyvia Rodríguez Del Valle,
Alejandro Cotté Morales, and Theresa Williamson

This chapter is the result of a collaborative research project between a nongovernmental organization based in Rio de Janeiro, Catalytic Communities, and Latin America's first community land trust — one of the world's only CLTs in an informal settlement—the Fideicomiso de la Tierra del Caño Martín Peña in San Juan, Puerto Rico. The aim of the research project was to study the potential of CLT instruments and strategies developed by the communities along the Martín Peña channel as a way to tackle insecure tenure in Rio's favela communities.[1]

Based on this research, we present recommendations on essential lessons when considering the creation of a community land trust in informal settlements, such as those that exist in Puerto Rico, Brazil, and most countries in the Global South. For the purpose of this essay, we have defined "informal settlements" as those where settlers have self-built homes in communal areas, on land to which they lack legal ownership, and on which they continue to live.[2] Many of these settlements have existed for several generations. Over time, therefore, they may become *consolidated*, whereby the building stock, access to some services, community ties, and a way of life have become firmly established, even as the residents' tenure has remained precarious; that is, their legal right to occupy the land beneath their homes has remained "informal." Regularization becomes a primary objective in these cases, the process to legally secure the occupancy and use of the lands underlying an informal settlement.

In this chapter, we identify a set of conditions that we have concluded must be in place in an informal settlement before considering the creation of a CLT as a primary land tenure and regularization strategy. We also present an analysis of legal strategies that we deem necessary to implement CLTs, specifically in the favelas (the informal settlements) of Rio de Janeiro. Our hope is that this chapter can serve other communities, organizers, and professionals who are interested in understanding the process of establishing a community land trust in an informal settlement.

There are very special elements to take into account in the creation of CLTs in the Global South, specifically in the context of informal settlements. The challenges of establishing a CLT in an informal settlement are quite different from those that are faced by CLTs in North American, British, and European cities. In those cities, new homes are usually being developed by a CLT at great financial cost, either through construction or rehabilitation, and then marketed to prospective homebuyers or renters who choose whether they want to come and live in this newly created housing. Before moving in, they can weigh whether living on land that is owned by a CLT and whether purchasing homes with limits on equity at resale will be acceptable to them. In informal settlements, by contrast, residents may in effect already own their homes, which were built by themselves or by previous generations. They often feel a sense of ownership of the underlying land, even when lacking legal documentation of their right to that land. Residents may be reluctant to share control over the land with a new organizational entity under a form of tenure that is foreign to them.

The type of organization we will discuss and propose here is designed, in part, to address such reluctance. A CLT in Brazil, therefore, like the one in Puerto Rico, would have to be organized and directed by community residents themselves in order to be successful.

In informal settlements across Latin America, especially in Brazil, there is an urgency to finding new strategies for securing land tenure. About half of Brazil's territory is estimated to lack full property rights (Ministério das Cidades, 2019). The legal precariousness of land tenure in the favelas has allowed arbitrary evictions by governments, like the many evictions that preceded two international sports events in Rio: the 2014 World Cup and the 2016 Olympic Games. The precariousness of tenure has also served as an excuse for governments to neglect the development of local infrastructure and the provision of adequate public services. Security of tenure and the regularization of land rights in the favelas thus become essential for realization of the right to secure, fully serviced neighborhoods and the right to the city (Soares Gonçalves, 2009).

Land regularization programs that have emphasized individual titling, where deeds to lands that were once occupied informally are conveyed to individual occupants, have often increased the risk of involuntary displacements, a result of market pressures that intensify in the wake of the legalization of land tenure. Even where forced evictions are not being implemented or where governments have invested public resources in on-site

Fig. 8.1. Fogueteiro favela, Central Rio de Janeiro. CATALYTIC COMMUNITIES

rehabilitation and upgrading programs, centrally located favelas face gentrification. In Rio, during the pre-Olympic period, gentrification, locally called *remoção branca*, or "white eviction," was widely reported in the local and international press, and debated during community events.

It is thus time to expand the conversation around land tenure beyond the legal aspects of land titling, and move away from the emphasis on individual ownership as the strategy for land regularization in informal settlements. Individual ownership has not protected informal communities from involuntary displacement and gentrification. The strategy to regularize land tenure must not be framed solely on "legalizing" how each individual relates to the parcel of land they occupy. Rather, it should be chosen by the residents themselves as part of a participatory process that helps them to move towards their vision for the future of their community. Land titling should not be an end in itself, but rather an instrument to achieve both collective and individual objectives. Such a process implies that there are options beyond individual titles, and that such options should be evaluated by the residents in accordance with their own priorities. A participatory approach of planning – action – reflection becomes the key to addressing land tenure.

This chapter starts with an overview of the situation in Rio de Janeiro's favelas today, where land insecurity has led to threats of eviction and gentrification. We describe past and present policies of land regularization in Brazil, arguing that these policies have not been able to put an end to involuntary displacements, which is why looking at mechanisms and policies that favor community ownership of land is a matter of great urgency. We then focus on the Fideicomiso de la Tierra del Caño Martín Peña, describing how residents of the Caño communities came to the conclusion that a community land trust was the best strategy to protect lands they and their families have inhabited for almost a century.

Finally, drawing upon lessons and insights we have gained from peer-to-peer exchanges between community leaders and staff of the Caño CLT in Puerto Rico and community leaders and technical supporters in Brazil, we present the legal implications for the establishment of a CLT in Rio de Janeiro's favelas. We then provide an analysis of conditions that must be present to make organizing a CLT both possible and feasible and we offer recommendations for community leaders, organizers, and supportive professionals to consider when taking the first steps toward creation of a CLT in an informal settlement.

I. RIO'S FAVELAS: INSECURE HOMES ON INSECURE LAND

Rio de Janeiro today has over 1000 favela communities, ranging in size from a handful to over 200,000 residents. Over 24% of the city's population lives in favelas, which constitute the city's primary affordable housing stock. The first community to be called a "favela" is today known as Morro da Providência (Providence Hill). The community's founders were formerly enslaved Africans who were recruited to fight in the bloody war of Canudos in Brazil's arid Northeast. They had been promised land in Rio de Janeiro, the nation's capital at the time, as payment for their military service. When they arrived in Rio in late 1897, however, no land was made available, so they settled on a hillside between the city center and the port. They named the hill "Morro da Favela" (Favela Hill) after the robust, spiny and resilient *favela* bush that dotted the hillsides of Canudos. Eventually, all of Rio's informal settlements — including ones settled long before, such as the community of Horto (settled in the early 1800s, still standing and fighting eviction today) — became known as favelas.

There are a number of facts essential to understanding why, over 122 years after the first favela was settled, the potential for Favela CLTs is currently galvanizing local organizers. First is the *scale* of the challenge. Rio's 1000 favelas today house over 1.4 million people, the vast majority of whom have no legal title for the land they occupy.

Second is the role of *race.* Rio was the largest slave port in world history and received five times the number of enslaved Africans as the entire USA. Slavery also lasted in Brazil 60% longer. Free men, who had previously been enslaved, had served in the bloody Canudos battle on behalf of their adopted nation. Denied their promised compensation, they squatted on land, starting a favela next to Rio's Port. Across the city, hundreds of thousands of other descendants of enslaved people and rural migrants joined them over

Fig. 8.2. Morro da Providência today, Rio's first favela. CATALYTIC COMMUNITIES

the following generations. As a result, today's racial maps of Rio show that black and mixed-race Brazilians tend to live in favelas, particularly in distant ones, while white Brazilians live mostly in upscale and centrally located regions.

Third is the historical *longevity* of these informal settlements. Rio's favelas, on average, are not the precarious "shanties" or exodus-desiring "slums" they are depicted as being in the mainstream media. Rather, they are well-established communities with a long history and a strong local cultural production and community investment.[3]

Finally, it is necessary to understand the intentional *neglect* inflicted on these communities. After 120 years, favela neighborhoods continue to be underserviced, over-policed, and insecure in their tenure. Rio is not a city that is only now beginning to urbanize. This happened decades ago, providing ample time for quality upgrades which never materialized.

Favelas Today: Products of a Cycle of Legitimized Neglect

One might argue that, at the outset, the founding of an informal settlement constitutes a failure of government, especially the failure to produce affordable, livable housing and a supportive neighborhood environment. Once consolidated, however, the real failure is to deny communities recognition, preservation, and improvement on their historic investment. When residents value their community and identify their *permanence* in the territory as a primary goal, however — not to mention when they have established a solid stock of self-built housing and other community amenities — this is a clear sign of a consolidated community or one that is on the path to consolidation. At this point, public policy should focus on identifying such communities and working with residents to detect needs and provide the services they lack, along with preserving community-built assets. In self-built communities, only residents are capable of accurately identifying their assets and needs and how best to preserve them and to address them. Thus, the need for community control over development becomes increasingly critical and just.

This realization has been recent. It came over the past decade, after Rio de Janeiro was selected the host city for the 2014 World Cup and the 2016 Olympics. Prior to 2008, the city had experienced economic stagnation for thirty years, and it was often assumed that underinvestment was due to a lack of public funds. During the Olympic build-up, however, the government spent over US$20 billion on infrastructure and other public improvements in Rio. Promises that were made to the favelas fizzled — including the Morar Carioca program which was supposed to upgrade all favelas by 2020 (Osborne, 2013). Instead, 77,000 favela residents lost their homes to forced evictions (Children Win, 2016).

In a handful of other favelas, the government gave out land titles and invested in policing to bring down crime rates. It also invested in formalizing public services (water, electricity) and community businesses. Community moto-taxi stands and other informally operated businesses now had to be registered, with associated fees and taxes paid up. That was also the case of access to critical utilities. Not coincidentally, this happened in favelas located in the city's touristy South Zone where land values are highest, and where eviction is the most politically difficult. These communities consequently experienced the beginning processes of gentrification, with the cost of living increasing, property values

Fig. 8.3. Vidigal favela, Rio's most notably gentrifying favela. FELIPE PAIVA

skyrocketing, renters leaving, hotels and bar chains opening up, and some homeowners selling, unaware that the value of their homes was monetarily (and emotionally) much greater than what they ended up accepting (Timerman, 2013).

It was at this point, and with the added support of community and international media (which replaced previous dependence on local media monopolies), that the government's policy of neglect and exploitation became explicit. A public official, unaware of the implications of his own comments, noted in 2013 that, "Favelas in the South Zone were fine when they provided cheap labor nearby. Not anymore." Residents of favelas are meant to serve, in other words, not to be served, or so it seems. When they are no longer useful, they need to move. When their land becomes valuable, they need to move. Such is the logic that permeates public policy and social relations across Rio's territory.

Favela organizers today are much more aware that what they are now experiencing and have always known is a vicious cycle of legitimized neglect. This has been the default policy of municipal and state governments toward favelas over generations. Lack of investment in the triad of services most-needed by communities (health, education, and sanitation) produces lack of opportunity and marginalization by the wider society, which in turn propels some residents toward criminal activity. This also makes favelas easy targets for criminal activity. When neighborhoods become known for crime, officials further justify their repressive actions, neglect, and evictions. And the cycle continues.

Despite this cycle, however, residents have built many resilient and culturally vibrant communities with immense potential. In Rio, favelas are also generally well-located across the urban fabric, most having been founded due to nearby employment and services. It is this patrimony they seek to defend and to build upon when residents insist that they want to remain in their neighborhoods. And this is why a tension surfaced during the pre-Olympic period: at the same time as communities facing eviction were being denied the titles they desired, communities facing gentrification spoke against individual titling. How could this be? Because titles, long thought to be a panacea, clearly didn't offer the type of protection that communities desired (Williamson, 2015).

Looking at land tenure alternatives is thus particularly urgent in the context of Rio de Janeiro. Instead of adopting mechanisms that offer the "right to speculate," favela organizers are searching for mechanisms that ensure the right to stay, along with greater access to public services, recognition of self-built community assets, and community control.

The Failure of Regularization Policies in Solving the Problem of Land Insecurity in Brazil's Favelas

More than fifty percent of Brazil's national territory is occupied in an informal or irregular way; that is, without formal title to the land. This started during Portuguese colonialism in the 16th Century. The change of this situation was only pursued in the 19th Century with enactment in 1850 of the Law of Lands.[4] Despite this legislative change, the scenario of uncontrolled land occupation continued, aggravated by a strong urbanization process that began in the 20th Century. Decades passed following passage of the Law of Lands, with no progress being made toward regularizing tenure in informal settlements. Nor were any new legislative or practical measures undertaken to solve the problem.

This scenario of neglect finally began to change in the urban context with the enactment of the Federal Constitution of 1988. It included a chapter dedicated to urban policy, the result of pressure applied by various social and technical movements in a struggle for urban reforms. This chapter of the Constitution would later be regulated by Federal Law 10.257 (2001), known as the City Statute, which introduced an important set of instruments for land regularization, providing a general guideline for national urban policy.

Despite growing attention to the problem of land insecurity in the form of legislation, land regularization as a public policy with wide-ranging pretensions was only instituted as a result of Law 11.977 (2009). This Law provided a basis for regularization of tenure that was focused on guaranteeing rights to the inhabitants of informal settlements and increasing the accountability of developers and real estate agents who contributed to the situation of land informality. The Law created a framework for land regularization, including provisions for the legal title and land registry for the lands occupied by residents of informal settlements. The Law also provided for territorial improvements and increased construction safety, and included measures aimed at improving social and economic conditions for residents of the country's favelas.

> Where land is most valuable, individual titling strengthens speculative investment.

Law 11.977 (2009) had little impact, however, because of its short duration. Its chapter on land regularization was revoked by Law 13.465 (2017), enacted after President Dilma Roussef was ousted from power. The new legislation altered the previous land regularization model, reducing it to a focus solely on the registration aspect; that is, the granting of title deeds to residents living in informal settlements. This Law emphasized individual titling through full private ownership, prioritizing registry regulation to the detriment of other dimensions of land regularization, especially those related to infrastructure improvements in the favelas and social assistance to residents, which had been essential components of the previous legislative framework, Law No. 11.977 (2009).

The most direct threat to the security of tenure came from the option given to the Brazilian legislature under this new law to distribute property titles to residents of informal settlements. In areas of the city where land is most valuable, individual titling strengthens speculative investment in real estate and increases the cost of living for the poorest residents. The increase in the cost of living is due to the introduction of (often exorbitant) fees for basic services such as water and electricity, the collection of property taxes, the forced formalization of local businesses, and the growth in new local businesses targeting a higher-income clientele. Meanwhile, the introduction of speculative development stimulates property sales by residents, which typically take place at values below the formal market rate, but above the values practiced in the informal market where properties were previously traded.

Nevertheless, like every policy intervention before it, this latest piece of legislation for land regularization has been marked by disputes and contradictions. Because it will fuel speculation, this new law directly threatens the security of tenure. It also denies the guarantee of low-income residents' right to services. On the other hand, this legal framework also makes it possible to mold a CLT, should full land rights be yielded to communities who want to create one. Careful monitoring of the implementation of this law is thus in order to ensure the security of the possession of the poorest.

II. ADAPTING INSTRUMENTS AND STRATEGIES OF THE CAÑO MARTÍN PEÑA CLT FOR POSSIBLE APPLICATION IN RIO'S FAVELAS

After ten years of work supporting hundreds of favela community organizers and then helping their communities to fight both government-sponsored evictions and market-led gentrification — one due to the absence of land titles and the other to their presence — Catalytic Communities (CatComm), a Rio de Janeiro-based nonprofit organization, began studying the potential of CLTs for Rio de Janeiro's favelas. In the early 2010s, the organization engaged with a number of academic and business partners who were familiar with the CLT model in the United States, theorizing and imagining its possible application to favelas. CLTs seemed to offer a solution that would support the residents of consolidated favelas in achieving their primary land security objective: *permanence*, the ability to stay put in neighborhoods where they are financially and emotionally invested, places where they feel a sense of belonging.

Fig. 8.4. Asa Branca favela street life. CATALYTIC COMMUNITIES

CLTs seemed to CatComm like they might be a good fit for formalizing Rio's favelas because a CLT is organized and operated along the same lines as a favela: homes are built, bought, inherited, and sold on a parallel, affordable housing market, while the underlying land is seen as a common good. Meanwhile, residents work collectively to build and to maintain their community and to fight for improvements. Favelas are often on land that is publicly owned. These informal settlements are regarded as providing for the "social function" of land, as required by Brazil's Constitution. CLTs can guarantee the security of land tenure of vulnerable populations, while also retaining the non-monetary values that residents have often built in their communities. This is done through a flexible arrangement that is easily adapted to different local realities. But it is also an emancipatory arrangement, since all planning and management of the territory arises from the residents, who are now in a position to officially define development within their own territory.

Despite suspecting that CLTs might have potential for formalizing Rio's favelas, however, Catalytic Communities did not feel capable of introducing something so unfamiliar and theoretical into the public debate. The mental leap required to take a North American model in which CLTs are built from scratch, and applying it to decades-old informal settlements in Brazil, building demand (and power) in the favelas for adopting this model, seemed an impossibility.

It was in this context that CatComm learned of the Caño Martín Peña CLT in Puerto Rico. Not only did seven San Juan communities successfully make this mental leap, they also *realized* a vision of what informal settlements could achieve when building upon the basics of the North American CLT model and creating a CLT to fit their own circumstances. The Caño CLT had successfully demonstrated that establishing CLTs in Rio's favelas might be an effective strategy to halt forced evictions,

> The CLT could function as an instrument of emancipation and empowerment.

while also addressing the challenges that typically come with individual land titles. These challenges include: higher costs of living, real estate speculation, and gentrification; individualistic thinking and the atomization of community; and a change in local culture due to the growth of *lógica mercadológica* (market-oriented logic), circumventing the traditional collective and demonetized exchanges on which favelas have historically been based. Community organizers in Rio's favelas typically spend so many years seeking individual titles as the primary solution to land insecurity that they rarely think about the brand-new set of challenges that await residents once those titles are issued. It is then too late to tackle these new challenges, since the mechanisms that might support resistance have by then been blunted through the introduction of the individualized logic of conventional titling.

The CLT, by contrast, seemed to offer a solution to *both* the first challenge (land security) *and* these secondary challenges. The CLT was not simply an arrangement for owning and managing land. As the Caño CLT had shown, it could also function as an instrument of emancipation and empowerment. The Caño CLT had demonstrated a growth in *unity* among seven neighborhoods as they participated in the community planning process that led to the establishment of their CLT, resulting in an incredibly rare level of *power* in their relationships with public authorities.

Caño Martín Peña CLT: Latin America's First CLT

For approximately 80 years, nearly 25,000 residents of the communities along the Caño Martín Peña (Martín Peña Channel) were invisible to government officials, at both the local and state levels. These communities, located in the heart of San Juan, Puerto Rico's capital city, were the result of rural migration during the economic crisis of the 1920s through the 1950s. Impoverished peasants moved with their families to the San Juan area looking for jobs and better living conditions. Most self-built their own housing. A number of families occupied dry land, but many built their homes on the wetlands along the Martín Peña Channel using cardboard, tin, and wood. A great number of them built their houses literally on the water. Over time the families and the municipal government filled the wetlands with all kinds of debris, creating dry land to sustain their makeshift homes. The city continued to grow, and soon the Caño communities found themselves in the heart of San Juan, next to its financial district. A place that no government administration wanted to look at or to care for became strategically located on valuable land that presented manifold development opportunities for the city and the country.

Government disinvestment and neglect, along with poor watershed management, led to a clogged channel. This was coupled with lack of adequate infrastructure, exposing residents of the Caño communities to an unhealthy environment. In 2002, however, after decades of studies and a lack of concrete action, the government announced its intention to dredge and to restore the Martín Peña Channel, reconnecting the lagoons, canals, wetlands, and beaches that are part of the San Juan Bay Estuary.

Having faced evictions and displacement in the past, residents of the Caño's communities inserted themselves into the planning process of what became the Caño Martín Peña Special Planning District in order to protect the permanence of their communities. They created the ENLACE Caño Martín Peña Project to spearhead the effort, completed with a strong community organizing and participation component.

Their participation turned an engineering project (unaware of its negative externalities) into a comprehensive development project (taking action to prevent such externalities) and led to the creation of public policy and institutions to make it feasible. Not only would the channel be cleaned and dredged, but improvements in stormwater and sewerage infrastructure were also planned in order to avoid further contamination, along with needed upgrades to the potable water and power infrastructure. It was recognized, too, that interventions would be needed to improve the quality of public spaces and inadequate housing, along with a sensible relocation strategy and socio-economic development initiatives.

The Comprehensive Development and Land Use Plan for the Caño Martín Peña Special Planning District (Development Plan), created with the active and informed participation of the residents, made it clear that for its implementation to be possible the community had to have control of the land. Of the approximately 188 hectares (466 acres) that comprise the Planning District, 78 hectares (194 acres), were scattered throughout and were owned by five different governmental entities. Although there were some vacant lots and public buildings, most of this acreage was occupied by residents lacking any kind of land title. The planned eco-restoration of the channel and rehabilitation of the District's infrastructure would have made these residents vulnerable to involuntary displacement and gentrification. That is why the Caño's communities held a long and thorough deliberation process to assess what kind of land ownership strategy might be available that would ensure the permanence of their communities (Algoed, Hernández-Torrales, Rodríguez Del Valle, 2018).

Within the Caño Martín Peña Special Planning District there had previously been different strategies and experiences regarding land ownership. At the beginning of this informal settlement, the peasants who occupied government-owned and publicly owned land without legal title became owners of the improvements on the land, but the land continued to be public or under the government's ownership.[5] During the 1960s and early 1970s, some of the Caño communities, with the government's assistance, formed land cooperatives that allowed many residents to acquire the land they occupied and to develop basic infrastructure for their communities. On July 1, 1975, the Puerto Rico Legislature enacted a law that made it possible for low-income families or individuals without land title, like residents of the communities along the Caño, to be able to acquire the title to public land at a very low cost, mostly for just one dollar (US$1.00). This measure was used by politicians as a clientelist strategy, however, to gain electoral votes and not all community residents benefited from the law.

By the year 2002, there were homeowners in the Caño communities who had individual title to their land, but almost fifty percent of the Caño's residents were still living on land over which they had neither ownership nor control. Residents realized that, because of the strategic location of their neighborhoods, restoring the Caño would further encourage the sale of plots of land with titles to speculators at higher prices than their market value, but significantly below their market potential, and continue to fragment the communities. Those who sold their plots would not be able to find alternative housing within the city for the money they had received for their land.

As part of the participatory planning, action, and reflection process that led to the eventual adoption of the Development Plan, residents evaluated various options to address insecurity of tenure against a set of priorities that included: avoiding displacement and gentrification as an unintended consequence of restoring the Caño; getting access to credit; and ensuring their heirs could inherit the right to occupy and use the land, supported by a valid title. Residents considered those forms of land ownership they already were familiar with, such as individual land titles and land cooperatives, and also explored ways of owning and managing land that were new to Puerto Rico, including the community land trust.

After thorough consideration, they found the CLT to be an instrument that is flexible enough to fulfill their needs and more. Three basic characteristics distinguished the CLT from other forms of ownership, namely community-led development on community-owned land for the provision of afford-

> The Caño's residents designed a CLT that would enable them to achieve security of tenure.

able housing for low-income families. Within that general framework, the CLT could be adapted and applied in any way a community might prefer. In the Caño's case, the residents concluded that a CLT would allow them to have collective control over the land and would ensure implementation of the Development Plan, including providing housing for families in need of relocation. The Caño's residents designed a CLT that would enable them to achieve security of tenure and to regularize their relationship with the land beneath their houses. Through the *Fideicomiso de la Tierra del Caño Martín Peña*, their right to use the land would be validated through a legal document (a deed) that recognized their right to use the surface of the land; that right would be inheritable under Puerto Rico's laws; the improvements (the house) would be registered at the Puerto Rico Registry of Real Estate Property, together with the surface rights deed; residents would be able to develop new housing; and they would have access to mortgage credit, among other important benefits they had not previously enjoyed.[6]

The Legal Framework of the Caño Martín Peña CLT

The CLT is a variable tool, allowing wide possibilities of adaptation according to the conditions of the legal system of each country. Puerto Rico was a Spanish colony until it was invaded by the United States in 1898. This caused a change of jurisdiction in legal terms. In the areas of private law (e.g., persons, property ownership and its modifications, different ways of acquiring ownership, obligations and contracts), Puerto Rico still applies fundamentals of the Spanish Civil Code, as do most Latin American countries. However, in areas such as corporate law, administrative law, and constitutional law, Puerto Rico uses the Anglo-Saxon common law as a primary reference.

Securing community control of the Caño's publicly owned land was critical for the implementation of the Development Plan and to provide housing for those residents who needed to be relocated to provide the physical space for the infrastructure projects. The costs of all the work planned for the dredging of the channel and rehabilitation of the Caño communities was initially estimated at $700 million, but Puerto Rico soon started to suffer from a severe economic and fiscal crisis that has now extended for more than fifteen years. Hence, in order to ensure the implementation of the Development Plan and to alleviate costs, it was essential not only that all public land within the Special Planning District would be put under the control of the organized communities, but that the cost to the communities of acquiring the land would be negligible. Otherwise, the cost of completing the Caño infrastructure projects would be rendered unbearable.

These considerations led the organized communities of the Caño to decide not to create the Caño CLT as a nonprofit corporation under the Puerto Rico General Corporations Law. Instead, the Caño communities decided to draft a bill that would create their CLT as a trusteeship, along with all the other instruments needed for implementation of the Development Plan. Among the other purposes of this innovative strategy, enactment of this special law by the government of Puerto Rico would enable the free transfer of public land to the Caño CLT.

Law 489-2004, as amended, gave life to the *Proyecto ENLACE del Caño Martín Peña* as an independent project. It also created the tools needed for its implementation. The legislation created a government corporation, the ENLACE Project Corporation (ENLACE). This new corporation was charged with responsibility for coordinating the dredging of the Martín Peña Channel. It would also be responsible for coordinating the rehabilitation and new construction of infrastructure (stormwater and sanitary sewers, potable water systems), the relocation of power lines, streets, and public spaces, and the relocation of families and housing. These interventions were deemed crucial not only for the ecological restoration of the channel, but also to reduce the risk of flooding with polluted water that recurrently affected the communities. The ENLACE Corporation was charged with creating the conditions for the economic and social development of the Caño communities as well.[7]

The Fideicomiso de la Tierra del Caño Martín Peña (Caño Martín Peña CLT) was also created by means of Law 489-2004 as a private legal entity, separate from ENLACE or from any other governmental agency or instrumentality, and was invested with the legal authority to fulfill its responsibilities. All the public land within the Special District was transferred by this Law to ENLACE, which then transferred the land to the CLT by means of public deeds.

The Caño Martín Peña CLT is governed by regulations and by a board of trustees designed by the residents as a result of a two-year participatory planning process. The composition of this board differs somewhat from the three-part model used by most CLTs in the United States. Residents of the Caño communities decided that they would retain a majority of the seats on the governing board, while still providing for representation by the government and by other parties who are not residents of the Caño. The CLT's eleven-member board of trustees is constituted as follows: four are individuals residing on CLT land, elected by their peers; two are community residents, delegated by G-8, a coalition of community-based organizations representing all of the Caño's neighborhoods; two are experts, selected by the board, according to the organization's needs; two are representatives of governmental agencies;[9] and one is a representative of the municipality of San Juan.

A Proposed Legal Framework for Brazilian CLTs

The Caño Martín Peña CLT provided the comparative starting point for Catalytic Communities' own research into how a CLT might be established in Brazil. As CLT practitioners around the world have discovered, the model and instruments developed in one country must be modified to conform to laws and politics in another country. That is true in the Brazilian case as well.

The trusteeship (*fideicomiso*) used by the Caño Martín Peña CLT, for example, which was established through an act of the legislature in Puerto Rico, cannot be used for the purpose of establishing a CLT in Brazil, unless a specific law were to be adopted. Any attempt to enact such a law would run into political and bureaucratic difficulties. Even so, CatComm and organizers in favela communities may eventually pursue the presentation of a CLT bill as a political strategy to foster debate on the issue. They would propose a model that is able not only to guarantee security of tenure, but also to integrate the community and to increase its capacity for self-management and political negotiation.

But, for now, an arrangement was sought using instruments already existing in the Brazilian legal system which are capable of providing the basis for the present-day implementation of a Brazilian model of the community land trust, tailored to local specifications and needs. A legal framework was developed and proposed by CatComm that unites several instruments for the construction of a community land trust that could be specifically applied to addressing the problem of land insecurity in the favelas of Rio de Janeiro. This legal framework for a Brazilian CLT has three components, which may be assembled sequentially in different stages or pursued on parallel tracks. They are as follows:

- Acquisition of land and regularization of title by community residents;

- Constitution of the legal entity to receive the land and to be responsible for the continuing ownership and management of the land; and

- Separation of ownership of buildings from the ownership of land, transferring surface rights back to community members who manage the legal entity that owns the land.

Land acquisition and regularization. The legal reality in Rio's informal settlements, as well as in favelas throughout Brazil, is of people occupying land for which they have neither ownership nor control. Sometimes this land has not even been registered. Considering that the community land trust relies on gaining possession of land, where the ownership of lands and buildings will then be separated, the regularization and registration of title and the transfer of ownership are indispensable for the implementation of a CLT. There are many instruments for the regularization and conveyance of land in Brazil. The most significant in terms of dealing with land insecurity in informal settlements are adverse possession, concession of use, donation, purchase and sale, and land legitimization.

- *Adverse possession (usucapião)* is used for the acquisition of titles of property by populations residing on privately owned land. The basic argument is that the registered owners have failed to fulfill the social function of the property for a certain period of time, stipulated by law, during which the residents occupied the property and, as a result of continuous occupation over many years, they now have a legal claim to that land.

- *Concession of use* is an instrument that usually applies to publicly owned land, where it is not possible to apply adverse possession. This is an administrative contract that grants the use of a property for a certain period of time. Generally, in order to provide the instrument with more security, concessions have a 99-year term that can be extended for an equal period.

- *Donation* is an instrument through which public or private owners donate, free of charge, the land inhabited by low-income residents to said residents.

- *Purchase and sale* demands a financial contribution from the residents.

- *Land legitimization* is a new instrument provided by Law 13.465 (2017), which was intended to become the main land regularization instrument in Brazil. Applicable in public or private areas, it seeks to ensure private property for residents of informal occupations, be they low-income or otherwise.

Constitution of a legal entity. With the use of one of these instruments, once title is regularized and the ownership of land is poised to be conveyed to a community land trust, there must be a legal entity in place to constitute the CLT, receiving title and becoming responsible for the ownership and management of the land for years to come. This legal entity may take various forms (e.g. association, condominium, etc.) in accordance with the Brazilian legal system. A case-by-case analysis will be required to decide the best format in a specific situation. CatComm's analysis has recommended that each CLT be established as a nonprofit legal entity with a dual objective of holding and managing land on behalf of a particular favela and preserving its affordability for low-income residents.

Separating land ownership and building ownership. Once these other stages have been achieved, the ownership of any buildings already existing on the land when it was acquired by the CLT, and, typically, the ownership of future buildings constructed on the land, must be separated from ownership of the underlying land. (The legal entity that owns the land — i.e., the CLT — must, in turn, be collectively controlled by residents who live on the land.) When it comes to the separation of ownership, there are several instruments available in the Brazilian legal system. The most appropriate of them, as concluded by CatComm's analysis, will be the surface rights deed, similar to what is being used by the Caño CLT in Puerto Rico.

With the separation of ownership, the three components of the legal constitution of a Brazilian CLT would be put in place. The crafting of each component will then depend upon the objectives and needs of the communities that are building the model. What is presented here is only a basic legal framework, which offers several options suitable to serve the diverse needs that will present themselves in practice.

Coming to the end of this legal sequence, the CLT will be able to exert its full potential in the territory it has chosen to serve. Especially based on a collective management model designed by the community according to its own needs and specificities, the CLT will be able to recognize local realities and to strengthen community assets as it seeks territorial improvements.

This methodology releases any CLT implementation from the need to wait or to depend on the approval of enabling legislation, which could take years considering the unstable Brazilian political scene. That said, the fight for specific CLT enabling legislation should be pursued in parallel to the application of existing instruments described above, since legislative support could significantly facilitate, support, and boost efforts to establish favela CLTs.[9]

The CLT is seen by a growing number of favela leaders, NGOs, legal experts, practitioners, academics, and public servants in the urban planning and land titling fields in Rio, as a *ferramenta de costura*, a "seaming tool" that integrates and addresses diverse conclusions reached separately over the years by residents and supporters working on supportively addressing the problem of informality. CLTs provide a foundation for:

- securing the social function of land;

- realizing the need for land regularization;

- respecting the typology and self-management already inherent in favelas;

- promoting and preserving the affordability of housing;

- respecting people's sense of belonging and deeper concern for permanence (rather than seeing homes as a "speculative investment");

- recognizing the importance of community-controlled, participatory planning processes;

- guaranteeing a re-ordering of the community, so that services can be provided, consistent with a "do no harm" approach; and

▪ engaging technical expertise in support of community planning, rather than through top-down models.

III. GUIDELINES WHEN CONSIDERING A CLT AS A POSSIBLE STRATEGY FOR REGULARIZING LAND TENURE AND PROTECTING HOMES IN INFORMAL SETTLEMENTS

The collaborative research project that was conducted by CatComm and the Caño Martín Peña CLT involved peer-to-peer exchanges between community leaders and staff of the Caño Martín Peña CLT and interested favela communities and professionals during five days in Rio de Janeiro in August 2018. From that collaboration, we tentatively offer guidelines and recommendations for other communities that might be interested in implementing a similar strategy in their own territory.

It should be noted that every community is different and, therefore, every CLT will also be different. There is no universal recipe as to how to create one. Community residents design the bylaws, policies, priorities, and internal procedures, which will define the CLT and will be different for every new CLT in accordance with the community's particularities, circumstances, and needs. It is worth repeating, as well, that a CLT that is designed to address the challenges of regularizing land tenure in informal settlements will be organized and operated differently from a CLT freshly created to provide new housing in neighborhoods where ownership of the land is already formal(ized). Our recommendations are aimed, in fact, at neighborhoods like Brazil's favelas where people have

Fig. 8.5. Delegation from the Caño Martín Peña visiting the Barrinha favela, August 2018.
CATALYTIC COMMUNITIES

occupied land for years which they neither own nor control. In such settlements, activists who are interested in creating a CLT must consider two questions: What are the *conditions* that must be present to make a CLT feasible in an informal settlement; and what is the *process* that organizers must follow to make a CLT a reality?

Conditions: Where Might It Be Feasible to Establish a CLT in an Informal Settlement?

Community leaders and activists, public officials or others interested in developing CLTs should take into account that CLTs may not work in every community. For a CLT to be considered in the first place, as a possible strategy for addressing the need for regularization and upgrading in Rio de Janeiro's favelas — and, for that matter, in the informal settlements of many other countries — the following conditions need to be present:

- Consolidated communities are located on lands where residents perceive a threat — or experience the reality — of gentrification, forced eviction, or other human-induced involuntary displacement;

- A large percentage of families lack legal titles and want to address the problem of insecure land tenure;

- There is a possible path to acquiring title(s) to the land;

- Residents feel a strong sense of belonging and a desire to remain in their community; and

- There is a solid process of community organization in place, supported by organizations that are ready to accompany the community and that are able to provide technical assistance.

The experience of Puerto Rico and discussions to date in Brazil reveal that there are additional conditions that may be essential to the process of establishing a CLT in informal settlements. Amongst them are:

1. An organized community and mature leadership that fosters horizontal participation, new leadership and decision-making among all sectors, and that is willing to assume new responsibilities and to make a commitment that will last the life of the community.

2. Supportive organizations and technical allies that are prepared to: (a) accompany the community in strengthening an organizing process and, if necessary, to facilitate and to provoke difficult conversations that will ensure that the participatory planning, action, and continuous reflection process needed to choose and implement a CLT will be controlled by the community and have widespread participation; (b) engage

in dialogues with residents to help inform their decision-making process, where the technical allies are willing to both listen and to learn from the residents and to share their knowledge; and (c) help to strengthen and to complement the community and economic resources that are required to fulfill the community's development plan.

3. Community planning that comes first. CLTs that are designed to regularize land tenure must emerge and develop from existing resident desires and demands. Residents must come together to evaluate their options and make an active choice to adopt a CLT, and that CLT must provide a path to addressing their very real needs. Residents must also reach a broad understanding that some form of collective or community ownership of the land will best serve their needs and will allow them to accomplish their development objectives, both social and economic.

4. Communities that have a strong sense of belonging. The Caño's leaders made it clear that residents with this strong sense of belonging are those that are the most supportive of their own CLT, and that the pride in one's community and a strong sense of history can be strengthened and stimulated in the process or creating a CLT.

5. A legal entity that is controlled by the community, which can receive land rights as a means of collective or community ownership, along with the mechanisms to make the transfer a reality.

These five conditions are key to a successful CLT, but not all of them need to be present at the first moment of considering whether or not to form a CLT. In fact, several get put in place during the process of mobilization and reflection leading up to the decision to move forward in establishing this instrument. What should be emphasized and observed in every case of creating and applying a CLT in an informal settlement is community initiative and broad participation, both in the design of the CLT and in the definition of the goals to be achieved.

Process: How Might Residents Get Started in Establishing a CLT in an Informal Settlement?

As a result of the peer-to-peer exchanges between community leaders and staff of the Caño Martín Peña CLT and interested favela communities and professionals, a number of recommendations were made on essential steps to be taken when considering the formation of a new CLT in an informal settlement.

Start a process of community planning-action-reflection. Before anything else, residents have to decide whether a CLT is the right mechanism for land regularization in their community. A thorough process of planning with active and continuous resident participation is crucial to make informed decisions about the type of land tenure that will best serve their needs and, if it is decided that a CLT is the right mechanism, how the CLT will be established and governed and how the land will be managed as a collective asset to realize the community's vision. *A CLT is not an end in itself, but rather an instrument to achieve the goals of the community.*

In the Caño, residents engaged in a participatory planning–action–reflection process, where through concrete actions they could obtain short-term wins to keep the community engaged, and continuously reflect on their actions so as to learn from them and inform their planning process. Such a process can be started by residents, community leaders, community-based organizations, government agencies or NGOs. In every case, however, supportive technical allies must recognize their role as being one of helping to create the conditions that will enable residents to strengthen their organizations, to take control of the process, and to participate effectively.

Further recommendations for this participatory process include:

- Start small. Think from less to more. Sports or cultural events can help as a mobilizing method.

- Get residents involved who are influential in the community and who are trusted by a wide range of residents.

- Organize events where residents can think of their ideal community and define what they want their neighborhood to become.

- Develop and use popular education techniques such as street theater, comic books, videos, and others, and engage youth in their design and as communicators.

- Remember that it always seems impossible until it is done.

Create CLT structures, policies, and procedures. If it is decided that the CLT is the right mechanism to meet the needs of the community, residents need to decide how the CLT will function. The bylaws, policies, and activities of every CLT will be somewhat different. Residents must formulate what the shape and function of their CLT should be, which may change over time when conditions or contexts change. The organizational structures and operational priorities of other CLTs can be consulted as inspiration. (See, for example, the rules and regulations of the Caño CLT in "Reglamento General para el Funcionamiento del Fideicomiso de la Tierra del Caño Martín Peña," 2008.)

Technical assistance from professionals. NGOs, universities, or government will be necessary to support residents in achieving their goals. Professionals — social workers, urban planners, architects, engineers, lawyers — should support the process, not lead it. They are not the ones to provide answers to questions, as the knowledge lies within the community. Rather, they can help to expand possibilities. Social workers and community organizers that accompany the community can help facilitate discussions, find alternative ways to engage residents, promote critical thinking, and ensure that participation is productive and inclusive. Planners can help the community to keep a comprehensive perspective throughout the process. Engage experts after residents have defined what they need and what they want. If experts come too early or without proper orientation to promote a balanced dialogue, they may downplay the community, co-opt the process, or impose their own standards on communities.

Define the legal possibilities. After the community has defined what it wants, lawyers can get involved to guide the community through which legal instruments already exist that make the transformations legally possible. If certain legal instruments do not yet exist, they can be created to meet the needs of the community, or elements can be borrowed from other legal instruments. Also here, residents themselves must design these new legal instruments, with the help of lawyers (not the other way around). If elements are taken from existing legal instruments, it is essential to focus on the final goal and to make adjustments in the process in order to ensure the community's goal is reached. If members of a community have decided they want to hold their land collectively, for example, but their only legal option is to pass through individual titles first (as is currently the case in Brazil for publicly-owned lands), it will be necessary for residents to have reached a decisive conclusion to combine their titles under a CLT well prior to receiving those titles, and execute that decision immediately. Otherwise, speculation can curtail the process. Ideally, in this case, the CLT organization should be established in advance and be ready to receive those titles as soon as they are issued.

Strategize. The process to establish and to maintain a CLT requires continuous organizing and strategizing on how to choose partners and on how to communicate and to engage with third parties in order to achieve such objectives as securing the land, dealing with conflicts, and attracting resources, among others. Taking the time to stop and to reflect on the challenges and opportunities within and beyond the community is key to developing a successful path forward.

——

Community land trusts are always unique. The Caño CLT borrowed some elements from other CLTs, but residents and their allies also created many new elements completely from scratch in order to address the needs of their community and to find ways to make their CLT function properly within their own context. CLTs in Brazil will undoubtedly take on a whole new shape, and will differ from community to community, depending on the goals of residents and the circumstances of each community.

It is essential to remember, however, that there should never be discussions about the community — including discussions about forming a CLT — without the community being present. As organizers in informal settlements, from Johannesburg to Rio, often say: "Nothing for us, without us."

At the time this essay is being written, a working group comprised of 154 community leaders and technical allies has formed in Rio de Janeiro and is supporting the development of pilot CLTs in two communities that meet the conditions described above: the Trapicheiros and Esperança communities. This working group is also developing enabling legislative proposals and outreach materials to share the CLT model with other communities. Trapicheiros and Esperança have each embarked on the process of establishing their own CLT and are currently holding regular community social events and workshops, engaging residents in a participatory planning process towards forming a CLT.

The working group formed after the August 2018 visit by a delegation of five Caño Martín Peña CLT organizers, who came to Rio to share their story. This city-wide, multi-partner working group includes leaders from over twenty communities, land rights agents from the state, planners and lawyers from Rio's universities, public defenders, NGOs and others. Some of them traveled to Puerto Rico in May 2019 to participate in a peer-to-peer exchange hosted by the Caño Martín Peña communities. Community leaders and their support organizations from Argentina, Bangladesh, Barbuda, Belize, Bolivia, Brazil, Chile, Ecuador, Jamaica, Lebanon, Mexico, Peru, South Africa, and the United States came to San Juan learn more about the Caño CLT.

Seeds are being sown for new CLTs across the world. To be continued!

Notes

1. The study was financed by the Latin America program of the Lincoln Institute of Land Policy.

2. We are focusing here on the informal occupancy of land as an *urban* phenomenon. Throughout the world, however, there are also millions of acres of *rural* land that are occupied and used for housing, farming, grazing, and woodcutting by people who have no formal title to these lands.

3. In recent years, twelve favelas have opened museums documenting their histories. The social museology movement is growing.

4. The land law of 1850 established purchase-and-sale as a form of land acquisition in Brazil, breaking with the previous model that had recognized effective occupation of a territory as a criterion of acquisition. In addition, it provided for a system of land registration aimed at the formal regularization of the national territory, which was not applied in practice, however.

5. Original inhabitants built their homes themselves. Over time, as people moved on, houses were sold using informal documents or private contracts that clearly established that the buyer was only acquiring the house, not the land. Almost all of those documents stated that the land was public land. None of the documents were registered, however, which precluded buyers from accessing mortgage credit.

6. From a procedural perspective, the Caño Martín Peña opted for a surface rights deed, instead of a ground lease, for regularizing use of the land and for securing and registering a family's ownership of the house. A ground lease agreement may be used for other owners, however, like businesses or organizations established on the CLT's land.

7. This government corporation was set up with a sunset provision. It is scheduled to go out of business after twenty-five years.

8. One of these should be a board member of the ENLACE Project Corporation.

9. In effect, there are two possible legal ways to enable the formation of a CLT in informal settlements: (1) the approval of a specific law, detailing a CLT's application and creating legal instruments to put the CLT into effect; or (2) the use of instruments already existing in the legal system, combining several of them for the CLT's formation and operation.

References

Algoed, L., A. Cotté Morales, T. Fidalgo Ribeiro, M.E. Hernández Torrales, L. Rodriguez Del Valle and T. Williamson (forthcoming). Community Land Trusts and Informal Settlements: Assessing the feasibility of CLT instruments developed by the Caño Martín Peña communities in Puerto Rico for Favelas in Rio de Janeiro, Brazil. Working Paper. Cambridge: Lincoln Institute of Land Policy.

Algoed, L., M.E. Hernández Torrales and L. Rodríguez Del Valle (2018). El Fideicomiso de la Tierra del Caño Martín Peña: Instrumento Notable de Regularización de Suelo en Asentamientos Informales, Working Paper. Cambridge: Lincoln Institute of Land Policy.

Corporación del Proyecto ENLACE del Caño Martín Peña (2008). Reglamento general para el funcionamiento del Fideicomiso de la Tierra, Núm. 7587. San Juan: Departamento de Estado.

Children Win (2016). *Rio 2016 Olympics: The Exclusion Games. https://www.childrenwin. org/wp-content/uploads/2015/12/DossieComiteRio2015_ENG_web_ok_low.pdf*

Ministério das Cidades. Regularização Fundiária Urbana—Lei 13.465/17. Accessed March 12, 2019. *http://www.cohab.mg.gov.br/wp-content/uploads/2017/11/Reurb-out..pdf*

Osborne, C (2013). "A History of Favela Upgrades Part III: Morar Carioca in Visio and Practice (2008–2013)." *RioOnWatch*, April 2. *https://www.rioonwatch.org/?p=8136*

Robertson, D. and T. Williamson (2017). "The Favela as a Community Land Trust: A Solution to Eviction and Gentrification?" *Progressive City*, May 2. *https://catcomm.org/law-clt/*

Soares, G. R. (2009). "Repensar a regularização fundiária como política de integração socioespacial." *Estudos Avançados* Vol. 23 No. 66. http://www.scielo.br/scielo.php?script=sci_arttext&pid=S0103-40142009000200017

Timerman, J. (2013). "Is a Favela Still a Favela Once It Starts Gentrifying?" *CityLab*, December 2. *https://www.citylab.com/equity/2013/12/favela-still-favela-once-it-starts-gentrifying/7726/*

Williamson, T. D. (2015). "A new threat to favelas: gentrification." *Architectural Review*, May 30. *https://www.architectural-review.com/opinion/a-new-threat-to-favelas-gentrification/8682967.article*

Williamson, T. D. (2018). "Community Land Trusts in Rio's Favelas: Could Community Land Trusts in Informal Settlements Help Solve the World's Affordable Housing Crisis?" *Land Lines*, July 31. *https://www.lincolninst.edu/sites/default/files/pubfiles/land-lines-july-2018-full_2.pdf*

Williamson, T. D. (2020). "Favela vs. Asphalt: Suggesting a New Lens on Rio de Janeiro's Favelas and Formal City," *Comparative Approaches To Informal Housing Around The Globe,* edited by Udo Grashoff. London: UCL Press.

Williamson, T. D. (forthcoming). "Proporcionar seguridad de tenencia para los actuales habitantes del barrio," *Barrio 31,* los inicios de una operación transformadora, edited by Agustina Gonzalez Cid. Washington, DC: Inter-American Development Bank.

Williamson, T. D. (2017). "Rio's Favelas: The Power of Informal Urbanism." *Perspecta 50: Urban Divides,* M. McAllister and M. Sabbagh (editors). Cambridge: MIT Press, September.

Williamson, T. D. (2019). "The Favela Community Land Trust: A Sustainable Housing Model for the Global South," *Critical Care: Architecture and Urbanism for a Broken Planet,* Angelika Fitz and Elke Krasny (editors). Cambridge: MIT Press.

ABOUT THE CONTRIBUTORS

NELE AERNOUTS is an architect, urban designer, and researcher. She is a postdoctoral researcher at Cosmopolis and teaches in the MSc in Urban Design and Spatial Planning (SteR*) at the Vrije Universiteit Brussel. Her research interests include collective housing, social housing, and participatory planning, with a specific focus on underprivileged groups. During her PhD, she studied diverse forms of housing commons and land tenures in the Brussels Capital Region, such as community land trusts and housing cooperatives, focusing on spatial and participatory dimensions. Currently she coordinates a LivingLab project tackling the regeneration of large-scale social estates.

LINE ALGOED is a PhD researcher at Cosmopolis, Center for Urban Research at the Vrije Universiteit in Brussels and a Research Fellow at the International Institute of Social Studies in The Hague. She works with the Caño Martín Peña CLT in Puerto Rico on international exchanges among communities involved in land struggles. She is also an Associate at the Center for CLT Innovation. Previously, Line was a World Habitat Awards Program Manager at BSHF (now World Habitat). She holds an MA in Cultural Anthropology from the University of Leiden and an MA in Sociology from the London School of Economics.

JOSHUA BARNDT is Executive Director of The Parkdale Neighbourhood Land Trust, a nonprofit, community-based organization that acquires land for affordable housing, supportive housing, and community economic development in Toronto's Parkdale neighborhood. He is a co-founder of the Canadian Network of Community Land Trusts. He previously worked as Community Liaison Officer coordinating a community benefits agreement as part of the Lawrence Heights Revitalization. Earlier, he served as Communications and Campaign Consultant for the "Right to the City Alliance" in New York City. He holds an MS in Design and Urban Ecologies from the Parsons School of Design, The New School.

SUSANNAH BUNCE is an Associate Professor in the Department of Human Geography at the University of Toronto Scarborough, Toronto, Canada. She has researched community land trusts in cities since 2009 and was the principal investigator on a three-year research project that examined urban community land trusts in Canada, the United States, and the United Kingdom, funded by the Social Sciences and Humanities Research Council of Canada. Her research on CLTs has been published in international academic journals and in a recent monograph published by Routledge. She holds a MES Planning and PhD in Environmental Studies from York University, Toronto.

Alejandro Cotté Morales holds a PhD in Social Policy from the Graduate School of Social Work of the University of Puerto Rico, Río Piedras Campus, where he is an Adjunct Professor. He has 25 years of experience as a community social worker. From 1994 to 2002, he directed the Community Development Area of the Península de Cantera Project. In 2002, he became Director of Citizen Participation and Social Development for ENLACE and the Caño Martín Peña CLT. He was instrumental in guiding grassroots organizing and participation processes around those initiatives, as well as advising on comprehensive development.

John Emmeus Davis is a founding partner of Burlington Associates in Community Development, a national consulting cooperative. He was housing director in Burlington, Vermont under Mayors Bernie Sanders and Peter Clavelle. Community land trusts have been a prominent part of his professional practice and scholarly writing for nearly 40 years. His publications include *Contested Ground* (1991), *The Affordable City* (1994), *The City-CLT Partnership* (2008), *The Community Land Trust Reader* (2010), and *Manuel d'antispéculation immobilière* (2014). He co-produced the film, *Arc of Justice,* and is co-director of the Center for CLT Innovation (*https://cltweb.org*). He holds an MS and PhD from Cornell University.

Geert De Pauw has been active for more than 20 years championing the right to housing in Brussels as an activist and community worker. In 2008, following a study visit to the Champlain Housing Trust, he began advocating for the establishment of a CLT in Brussels. He coordinated the CLT feasibility study that was commissioned by the Brussels Capital Region. He has been a coordinator of the CLT Brussels since 2012. He was also a co-founder of SHICC (Sustainable Housing for Inclusive and Cohesive Cities), a European partnership whose goal is to create a thriving CLT movement in Europe.

Nate Ela is a visiting researcher at the American Bar Foundation. He recently received his PhD in sociology from the University of Wisconsin-Madison. He also holds a JD from the Harvard Law School. He is currently working on a book explaining why urban reformers have repeatedly turned to farms and gardens as a means of redistributing resources and supporting people in need. His writing on property, social policy, and human rights has appeared in *Law & Social Inquiry, Social Science History,* and the *Fordham Urban Law Journal.*

TARCYLA FIDALGO RIBEIRO is Co-coordinator of the Favela CLT program at Catalytic Communities in Rio de Janeiro and a researcher for the Metropolis Observatory, a project led by Rio de Janeiro's Federal University which encourages reflection about cities and urban planning in Brazil. She holds a Bachelor's Degree in Law and a Master's Degree in Urban Law from the State University of Rio de Janeiro. She has done post-graduate work in urban sociology and in urban planning and policy at the Federal University of Rio de Janeiro, where she is presently enrolled as a doctoral candidate.

ALAN GOTTLIEB is a Colorado-based writer, editor, journalist, and nonprofit entrepreneur with more than 20 years of experience in education policy and education journalism. Currently, Alan is owner of Write.Edit.Think.LLC, an independent communications consulting firm. Alan co-founded Chalkbeat, a growing and increasingly prominent national news nonprofit focused on PreK-12 education policy, policy implementation and practice. From 1988-97, he was a reporter and editor with *The Denver Post*. From 1997 until June 2007, he served as education program officer at The Piton Foundation in Denver. He is the author of two books, one fiction, one non-fiction.

MARÍA E. HERNÁNDEZ-TORRALES holds an LLM in environmental law from the Vermont Law School and an MA in Business Education from New York University. She studied for her undergraduate and Juris Doctor degrees at the University of Puerto Rico. Since 2005 she has been doing pro bono legal work for the Proyecto ENLACE and for the Fideicomiso de la Tierra del Caño Martín Peña. Since 2008, Hernández-Torrales has worked as an attorney and clinical professor at the University of Puerto Rico School of Law where she teaches the Community Economic Development Clinic.

TONY HERNANDEZ is the Director of Dudley Neighbors Inc., a community land trust established by the Dudley Street Neighborhood Initiative in 1988. DNI has combined community ownership of land, community control of development, and permanent affordability of housing to revitalize a large section of Roxbury that had long been scarred by vacant lots, abandoned buildings, and arson-for-profit. DNI's high-profile success in achieving "development without displacement" has inspired other communities to create CLTs of their own in Boston and elsewhere. Tony has been a CLT homeowner for the past 18 years. He has a Master's degree in architecture.

STEVE KING is Executive Director of the Oakland Community Land Trust in Oakland, California (*https://oakclt.org*). He has spent the past 15 years working for community-based organizations in the areas of equitable development, affordable housing, and applied social research. Steve previously served as the Housing and Economic Development Coordinator at the Urban Strategies Council, also based in Oakland. He holds a MS in Urban Planning from Columbia University, and a BA in Environmental Science from Boston University.

Aaron Miripol is a leader in nonprofit real estate development with a focus on growing CLTs for the benefit of local communities. Since 2007, as President of the Urban Land Conservancy, he has overseen 38 investments in Metro Denver, including multi-family affordable housing, schools, and commercial space. Prior to ULC, Aaron led Thistle Community Housing, increasing its portfolio from 100 to 1,000 permanently affordable homes, including 250 for-sale homes. In his career, Aaron has overseen $800M in affordable housing and community development. He gained an early appreciation for CLTs while working at Moshav Kerem Maharal, a cooperative farm in Israel.

Lyvia Rodríguez Del Valle is the former Executive Director of the Caño Martín Peña CLT and Corporación Proyecto ENLACE del Caño Martín Peña. For over 15 years, she worked with an interdisciplinary team and community organizations on implementation of the ENLACE Project. Lyvia previously worked on urban revitalization in San Juan and risk management and decentralization in Quito and Asunción. She holds a master's degree in Urban and Regional Planning and a graduate certificate in Latin American Studies from the University of Florida, Gainesville, and a bachelor's degree in Environmental Design from the School of Architecture, University of Puerto Rico.

Greg Rosenberg is Co-Director of the Center for Community Land Trust Innovation (*https://cltweb.org*) and a principal of Rosenberg and Associates, a consultancy focused on affordable and sustainable housing, cohousing, community land trusts, and urban agriculture. He was a founder of the CLT Network and the CLT Academy in the USA and served as the Academy's first director. He previously led the Madison Area CLT, where he developed Troy Gardens, an urban ecovillage featuring a working farm, community gardens, a restored prairie, and a 30-unit mixed-income cohousing project. Greg is licensed to practice law in Wisconsin and is a LEED Accredited Professional.

Dave Smith is a community organizer, affordable housing practitioner and writer, based in London, England. From 2008–2014, he served as the founding Executive Director of the London Community Land Trust, which is now the largest CLT in the UK. Prior to this, Dave worked for the British Council and on Barack Obama's 2008 primary and presidential election campaigns. More recently, he has worked at the National Housing Federation and is currently a freelance consultant and author. He holds degrees from King's College, the University of Cambridge, and The Bartlett School of Planning, University College London.

Harry Smith is a Community Development and Organizing consultant with 25 years of experience in the field. He most recently served as Director of Sustainable Economic Development for the Dudley Street Neighborhood Initiative, including managing the activities of Dudley Neighbors Inc., one of the nation's largest urban community land trusts. He currently works with a number of community-based organizations on projects related to community organizing, land use, strategic planning, and support for emerging CLTs. He earned a BA from Brown University and an MS in Community Economic Development from Southern New Hampshire University.

THERESA WILLIAMSON, PhD, is a city planner and founding executive director of Catalytic Communities, an NGO working to support Rio de Janeiro's favelas through asset-based community development. CatComm produces *RioOnWatch,* an award-winning local-to-global favela news platform, and recently launched Rio's Sustainable Favela Network and a Favela Community Land Trust program. Theresa is an advocate for the recognition of the favelas' heritage status and their residents' right to be treated as equal citizens. She received the 2018 American Society of Rio prize for her contributions to the city and the 2012 NAHRO Award for her contributions to the international housing debate.

www.ingramcontent.com/pod-product-compliance
Lightning Source LLC
Chambersburg PA
CBHW080557030426
42336CB00019B/3226

9 781734 403077